Ottolenghi

SIMPLE

Ottolenghi SIMPLE

A Cookbook

Yotam Ottolenghi with Tara Wigley and Esme Howarth

Photographs by Jonathan Lovekin

TEN SPEED PRESS
California | New York

Contents

Introduction: Ottolenghi

There are all sorts of ways to get a meal on the table, depending on the sort of cook you are. One person's idea of cooking simply is the next person's culinary nightmare. For me, for example, it's about being able to stop at my grocery store on the way home, pick up a couple of things that look good and make something within 20 or 30 minutes of getting home. My husband, Karl, on the other hand, has a completely different idea of what "simple cooking" is. If we're having friends over on the weekend, he'll want to spend a good amount of time beforehand, prepping and cooking as much as he can so that very little needs to be done when our guests are around.

There are other ways, too. Esme, who led the recipe testing for this book, prefers to be in the garden on the weekend rather than kitchen-bound. Her idea of simple cooking is to put something in the oven on a Saturday morning and leave it simmering away, ready to be eaten four or five hours later. Tara, on the other hand, who led the writing, can't really relax without knowing that a meal is basically ready a full day before it's due to be eaten. Sauces are in the fridge, stews are in the freezer, veggies are blanched or roasted and ready.

Whatever our approach, it all looks effortless and easy when friends and family come to eat in our respective kitchens. This is only because we've worked out the way that suits us to make cooking simple, relaxing and therefore fun. It's different for everyone. This idea, then—that there's more than one way to get a meal on the table and that everyone has a different idea of which way is simple—is what *Ottolenghi SIMPLE* is all about.

And, no, for anyone wondering, *Ottolenghi SIMPLE* is not a contradiction in terms! I know, I know: I've seen the raised eyebrows, I've heard the jokes. The one about the reader who thought there was part of a recipe missing as they already had all the ingredients they needed in their cupboard. Or the one that goes, "Just popping out to the local shop to buy the papers, milk, black garlic, and sumac!"

I hold up my hands, absolutely. There have been lists to make and ingredients to find but, truthfully, there's not a recipe to my name that I feel sheepish about. Cooking, for me, has always been about abundance, bounty, freshness, and surprise. Four big words to expect from a plate of food, so a single sprig of parsley was never, really, going to cut the mustard. The reason I'm so excited about *Ottolenghi SIMPLE* is that it's full of recipes that are still distinctly "Ottolenghi" but are simple in at least one (but very often in more than one) way.

To build on the different definitions of simplicity for different people, Tara devised a clear and practical color-coded system. The beauty of Tara's system is that it allows you, once you've figured out what kind of "simple cook" you are and for what kind of "simple occasion" you are cooking, to select the recipes that are right for you. Those bright colors are really there to help you plan meals and then make them, with minimum hassle and maximum joy.

short on time

With your ingredients in the house, your knife sharp, the oven on and the decks clear, these recipes will take less than 30 minutes to get on the table. Noodles and pasta dishes come into their own, with their short cooking time, as does fish, which is so often quick to cook. Meat can be speedy as well, though, with things like lamb patties and chicken schnitzel needing very little time in the pan. Raw vegetable recipes will nearly always be quick to make, as are half the brunch dishes, which is what you want when cooking in the morning.

The short-on-time recipes are the ones I eat for supper during the week and the recipes I feed friends for brunch on the weekend. They're the dishes that can be made so quickly and easily that, sometimes, I end up making five or six at once so that my plans for a simple meal turn, inadvertently, into a big feast.

10 ingredients or less

I thought that imposing a limit of 10 ingredients or less on my recipes was going to be a big challenge, but it was actually the biggest thrill. The temptation to add layer upon layer of flavor and texture is one I often happily fall for, but knowing that I couldn't do that here was a form of liberation.

The most thrilling thing of all, though, was the achievement of this for so many recipes without ever thinking that a recipe was in any way lacking. I can't see myself becoming a herb apologist in the future (green things make me happy!) and there's never a dish I regret squeezing lemon over—but, absolutely, less can be more and abundance can still be achieved with fewer ingredients.

So what have I left out that might have otherwise been there? One or two different herbs are used instead of three or four, for example. One type of oil or salt or variety of chile was shown to be enough. Some ready-made spice mixes—such as curry powder or Chinese 5-spice powder—were a great alternative to grinding and combining a host of individual spices. A dish was bold enough not to need the teaspoon of sugar, clove of garlic, or half teaspoon of dried mint or tomato paste I might have otherwise added. Rather than using vinegar and lemon, I'd use just one and increase the amount.

With the exception of harissa, though—one of my absolute pantry must-haves—and one recipe that has a tablespoon of sriracha in its dressing (see the prawn recipe on page 258), I decided not to rely on ready-made chile pastes, such as Thai green or red curry pastes. There are some really good pastes available but, as freshness is so important to me, I'd rather make a simple quick curry paste of my own, using a few key ingredients, than use an ingredient-packed ready-made version.

Ingredients I haven't included in the number count are: **salt, pepper, water, olive oil** and—in a handful of recipes—**garlic** and **onion**.

make ahead

Ottolenghi food is all about freshness. Herbs and leaves don't like to sit around after they've been chopped or dressed. A lot of baked things like to be eaten soon after they come out of the oven. There are all sorts of ways, though, to get ahead with the meal you're making without compromising on how fresh it is.

Many things, such as spreads and sauces, dips, and dressings, for example, are happy to be made a day or two ahead and kept in the fridge, ready to be warmed through or brought back to room temperature before serving. The freezer is also your friend. It's often as easy to double the amount of a pasta sauce or stew that a recipe calls for, for example, as it is to make the amount you need for one meal. That way you can just freeze half, have your next meal ready and waiting, and feel disproportionately pleased with yourself in the process.

It's not just about getting food into the fridge or freezer the day or week before, though. Making ahead also includes all the ways you can get ahead by a few hours on the day you're prepping for a meal, so that a dish is ready to be assembled when it's time to eat. Nuts can be toasted, batter mixed, stuffing prepped, grains cooked and refreshed, vegetables blanched and dried, or even (in the case of wedges of eggplant or squash) roasted in the oven and brought to room temperature. These are all things that can be done hours (or even the day) before. Herbs might not like to be chopped but the leaves can certainly be picked from the stems in advance. Just cover them with a slightly damp paper towel and keep them in the fridge, unchopped.

With meat, a lot can be done in advance. Meatballs can be made up and rolled (ready to be cooked when needed) or even seared in advance (ready to be warmed through before serving). Chicken thighs or beef sirloin can be marinating a day or two ahead of when you're ready to cook. Slow-cooked stews can be made a day or two ahead and then, again, warmed through before serving.

Desserts, as well, can very often be made ahead. Ice creams sit happily in the freezer, many cakes and most cookies keep well in an airtight container, and fridge cakes take up residence in, well, the fridge. Other times it's about elements that can all be made in advance, ready to be put together before serving (the cherries and crumble and cheesecake, for example, in the cheesecake on page 268), leaving a minute's worth of assembly to do before a knockout dessert is brought to the table.

The joy of make-ahead recipes is that, with the knowledge that most of the work is done, you can then actually be in the moment when it comes to serving and enjoying a meal. Having friends and family over is as much about hanging out together as the food that you eat, and there shouldn't be a big gap between the relaxed fun of planning a meal and the reality of making it happen. People don't go to their friends' house expecting food to be served *à la minute* and checked at the pass. That is what restaurants are for. If you're someone who likes to plan and get ahead, don't turn into a crazy-person chef the night your friends are coming over for supper.

pantry

What people have in their cupboard depends, obviously, on what they like to cook and eat. The fact that my cupboard shelves are always home to a tub of tahini, some green tea, and dark chocolate does not, I know, mean that anyone else's are going to be.

That being said, there are a few things I've assumed you will have on hand. If a recipe relies on them, then it will be seen as pantry-led. These everyday ingredients are:

everyday ingredients

Olive oil	Lemons	Canned beans
Unsalted butter	Greek-style yogurt	(lentils, chickpeas,
All-purpose flour	Parmesan (or pecorino)	lima beans)
Large eggs	Herbs	Canned tuna and
Garlic	Dried pasta	anchovies
Onions	Rice	Salt and pepper

You might still have to pick something up—a piece of fresh cod, for example, for the dish of chickpeas with flaked cod (page 262) or some spinach leaves for the gigli pasta (page 191)—but my thinking is that you'll be able to stop by just one shop on the way home rather than have to write a long list or go out of your way.

As well as these everyday ingredients, there are 10 "Ottolenghi" ingredients I'm assuming you won't have in your cupboard already, which I'm urging you to go out and buy. Simple cooking is often about injecting as much flavor as possible into a dish in a way that is quick and easy. These are some of my favorite little flavor bombs to help you to do that. They all have a long shelf life and are used again and again throughout the book.

"Ottolenghi" ingredients

Sumac	Pomegranate molasses	Black garlic
Za'atar	Rose harissa	Preserved lemons
Urfa chile flakes	Tahini	
Ground cardamom	Barberries	

For more on what these ingredients are, where to find the best version of them, and why they're so good to have in the cupboard, see page 299.

What you have in your cupboard changes, of course, according to the season. A dish of roasted mushrooms and chestnuts (page 112) is something you'll be able to magic up around Christmas in a way that you couldn't in the less festive months.

Pantry recipes are also meant to be versatile. My fridge-raid salad dressing (page 37), for example, uses the herbs that needed to be used up when making the recipe, but it's going to work as well without the tarragon and with a bit more basil, if that's what you have. The chocolate fridge cake (page 288) is about as robust as a dessert can be. I've suggested the dried fruit, chocolate flavor, and alcohol I like to add to the mix, but start with what you have in your cupboard and take it from there. There's something particularly satisfying about making a meal out of what you already have around.

lazy

Lazy cooks are busy off doing something else while the meal is making itself. These are the slow-cooked stews simmering on the stove while you're in the garden, the whole head of celery root you leave to roast in the oven for hours, the chicken legs that have been marinating overnight and now just need to be transferred to a baking dish in the oven and left to cook. All the work has been done beforehand, to ensure that the dish gets the flavor it needs, but then it's up to the combined forces of heat and time to do all the work.

These are also the one-pot or one-sheet pan dishes, low on washing up, high on ease, and big on flavor: the vegetables mixed with one or two things—carrots with harissa, for example, or mushrooms and chestnuts with za'atar—tipped onto a sheet pan and simply roasted.

These are the cakes that need no baking and the rice dishes that can be put into the oven in a baking sheet and forgotten about. These are the dishes that fill your house with smells, don't fill your sink with washing up, and allow you to get on with those jobs you never seem to get around to—or, alternatively, to delight in the possibility of actually being lazy and returning to bed with the paper.

easier than you think

Easy cooking, like simple cooking, depends on what kind of cook you are. One person's idea of easy is different than the next. Making your own bread, for example, is either something you grew up doing or, on the other hand, have never even contemplated. Pastries, ice cream, labneh, custard—they're all the same. Sometimes the simplest things—getting couscous or rice perfectly fluffy or an egg perfectly boiled—can floor one. The "E" recipes in this book will show you how much easier dishes can be than you think.

Other recipes that fall into this category are the ones that look or sound a bit restauranty but are actually super easy. The burrata with grilled grapes and basil (page 43), and the Trout tartare with browned butter, and pistachios (page 243) are examples. These both read as though they should be served in a high-end restaurant, but you'll be amazed by how easy they actually are. Don't be intimidated, also, by recipe names that have French or Italian words in them. Confit, carpaccio, and clafoutis all sound like you should only try the recipe if you've been to cooking school, but it's all just a ruse!

This is true of all cooking, really. Notwithstanding words in languages you might not speak, if you can read you can cook, and if you know what kind of cook you are—a make-ahead cook or a short-on-time cook or a whatever-I-have-in-my-cupboard cook—then things will be simpler still. None of us are one set type or the other, of course; we are all sorts of different cooks for all sorts of different occasions and times in our lives. My hope, though, is that for all those who want their food to remain abundant and bold but the cooking of it to be simple, the *Ottolenghi SIMPLE* structure here will be a kitchen liberation.

a note about ingredients, make-ahead recommendations, and oven temperatures

Unless otherwise stated: All eggs are large, all milk is whole, all weights in parentheses are net, all salt is table salt, black pepper is freshly cracked, parsley is flat-leaf, and all herbs are fresh. Onions are white, olive oil is extra-virgin, and lemon and lime pith are to be avoided when the zest is shaved. Onions, garlic, and shallots are all in need of peeling, unless otherwise stated. Preserved lemons are small. Belazu rose harissa has been used throughout the book; different varieties and brands of harissa vary greatly from each other so the instruction to increase or decrease the amount needed is always given. Flour is measured by scooping the cup into the bin and leveling with a knife.

When a recipe (or parts of the recipe) can be made ahead, estimates are given for how far in advance this can be: up to 6 hours, up to 2 days, up to 1 week, and so forth. Different conditions will affect how long something lasts, though—how long it has been kept out of the fridge, how hot the kitchen is, etcetera—so make-ahead recommendations must be weighed on a case-by-case basis as to whether something is still in good shape to eat. When instructed to keep something in the fridge, if made in advance, it will be best eaten once brought back to room temperature (or warmed through) rather than eaten fridge-cold.

We also recommend using an oven thermometer as all ovens will vary.

Brunch

Braised eggs with leek and za'atar

Serves six

2 tbsp unsalted butter

2 tbsp olive oil

2 extra-large leeks (or 4 smaller), trimmed and cut into ¼-inch/½cm slices (6 cups/530g)

salt and black pepper

1 tsp cumin seeds, toasted and lightly crushed

½ small preserved lemon, seeds discarded, skin and flesh finely chopped (2½ tbsp)

1¼ cups/300ml vegetable stock

7 oz/200g baby spinach leaves

6 large eggs

3¼ oz/90g feta, broken into ¾-inch/2cm pieces

1 tbsp za'atar

This is a quick way to get a very comforting meal on the table in a wonderfully short amount of time. It's a dish as happily eaten for brunch, with coffee, as it is for a light supper with some crusty white bread and a glass of wine. The leeks and spinach can be made up to 1 day ahead and kept in the fridge, ready for the eggs to be cracked in and braised.

1. Put the butter and 1 tbsp of the oil into a large sauté pan with a lid and place over medium-high heat. Once the butter starts to foam, add the leeks, ½ tsp of salt, and plenty of pepper. Fry for 3 minutes, stirring frequently, until the leeks are soft. Add the cumin, lemon, and vegetable stock and boil rapidly for 4–5 minutes, until most of the stock has evaporated. Fold in the spinach and cook for 1 minute, until wilted, then decrease the heat to medium.

2. Use a large spoon to make 6 indentations in the mixture and break 1 egg into each space. Sprinkle the eggs with a pinch of salt, dot the feta around the eggs, then cover the pan. Simmer for 4–5 minutes, until the egg whites are cooked but the yolks are still runny.

3. Mix the za'atar with the remaining 1 tbsp of oil and brush over the eggs. Serve at once, straight from the pan.

Pictured on page 4

Harissa and Manchego omeletes

I like to eat this either for brunch or for a speedy supper, with a fresh tomato and avocado salad on the side. The onions can be caramelized 2 days in advance and kept in the fridge, so it is worth making a double batch of these. Add a tablespoonful to scrambled eggs or couscous salad, for example. Make the egg mixture the day before if you like and let it sit in the fridge. Everything is then ready to be poured into the pan.

1. Preheat the broiler to high.

2. Put 3 tbsp of the oil into a medium (8-inch/20cm) ovenproof frying pan and place over medium heat. Add the onion and cook for 15 minutes, stirring from time to time, until the onion has caramelized and is a deep golden brown. Tip into a large bowl and add the eggs, milk, harissa, nigella seeds, half the cilantro, ½ tsp of salt, and a good grind of black pepper. Whisk to combine and set aside.

3. Wipe clean the pan you cooked the onions in, increase the heat to medium-high, and add 2 tsp of the oil. Pour in one-quarter of the egg mixture, swirling it around so that the mixture is evenly spread. After 1 minute, sprinkle with one-quarter of the Manchego and place under the broiler for 1 minute for the cheese to melt and the eggs to puff up and finish cooking. Using a spatula, ease around the edges of the omelete to slide it out of the pan and onto a plate. Keep warm while you continue with the remaining egg mix in the same way, adding more oil with each batch, to get 4 omeletes.

4. Serve at once, with the remaining cilantro sprinkled on top and a lime half alongside.

Serves four

5 tbsp plus 2 tsp/85ml olive oil

1 large onion, thinly sliced (2½ cups/250g)

12 large eggs, lightly beaten

7 tbsp/100ml whole milk

4½ tbsp/65g rose harissa (or 50 percent more or less, depending on variety; see page 301)

2 tsp nigella seeds

¾ cup/15g cilantro, roughly chopped

salt and black pepper

4 oz/110g Manchego, coarsely grated

2 limes, halved, to serve

Pictured on page 5

Zucchini and ciabatta frittata

This is a regular feature at home on the weekend, when Karl and I are feeding friends. We tend to serve it with a mixed herb and leaf salad dressed with lemon juice and olive oil and a few chunks of feta crumbled over it. The frittata manages to be light, fluffy, and comforting in a way that you can only get when you soak bread with milk and cream. Don't waste the ciabatta crusts: they can be blitzed into fresh breadcrumbs and freeze well. This can be baked about 4 hours in advance and then warmed through for 5 minutes before serving. Ideally it should be eaten on the day it is baked, but it will keep in the fridge for 1 day; just warm through for 10 minutes.

Serves six

1 lb 2 oz/500g ciabatta, crusts removed, roughly torn (6 cups/250g)

¾ cup plus 2 tbsp/ 200ml whole milk

¾ cup plus 2 tbsp/ 200ml heavy cream

2 large garlic cloves, passed through a garlic press

6 large eggs, lightly beaten

¾ tsp ground cumin

3 oz/80g Parmesan, finely grated

salt and black pepper

2 medium zucchini, coarsely grated (4 cups/430g)

1¼ cups/25g basil leaves, torn

2 tbsp olive oil

1. Preheat the oven to 400°F.

2. Put the ciabatta, milk, and cream into a medium bowl and mix well. Cover and set aside for 30 minutes, for the bread to absorb most of the liquid.

3. Put the garlic, eggs, cumin and ¼ cup/50g of Parmesan into a separate large bowl with ¾ tsp salt and ¼ tsp pepper. Mix well, then add the bread and any remaining liquid, followed by the zucchini and basil. Stir gently.

4. Place an 8 x 10-inch/20 x 25cm baking dish in the oven for 5 minutes, until hot. Remove from the oven, brush with the oil, and pour in the zucchini mix. Even out the top and bake for 20 minutes. Sprinkle the last of the Parmesan evenly on top of the frittata, then bake for another 20–25 minutes, until the frittata is cooked through—a knife inserted into the center should come out clean—and the top is golden brown. Set aside for 5 minutes, then serve.

Portobello mushrooms with brioche and poached eggs

As with all dishes that involve eggs and toast and getting ready in the morning, this is all about timing. Ideally, you want the mushrooms and toast coming out of the oven about the same time, and the eggs poached and ready soon after. Get the mushrooms cooking first, put the bread into the oven halfway through, and then get the eggs poaching. This works as well as a starter late in the day as it does in the morning. Use duck eggs for an extra-rich twist.

Serves four

14 oz/400g portobello mushrooms, sliced ½-inch/1cm thick

5 tbsp/75ml olive oil

2 garlic cloves, minced

½ tsp ground cinnamon

flaked sea salt and black pepper

¼ cup/5g basil leaves

⅛ tsp ground red pepper, plus extra to serve

4 slices of brioche, cut ¾-inch/2cm thick (about 5¼ oz/150g)

4 large eggs

⅓ cup plus 2 tbsp/ 100g sour cream, to serve

1. Preheat the oven to 450°F.

2. Mix the mushrooms with 3 tbsp of the oil, 1 garlic clove, ¼ tsp of the cinnamon, ½ tsp flaked salt, and a good grind of pepper. Spread out on a large parchment-lined baking sheet and roast for 15 minutes, stirring after 7 minutes, until soft and starting to brown. Toss with the basil and set aside.

3. While the mushrooms are in the oven, mix the remaining 2 tbsp of oil with the remaining ¼ tsp of cinnamon, 1 garlic clove, the pepper flakes, and ¼ tsp of flaked salt. Brush the oil and spices on one side of the brioche slices and place on a separate parchment-lined baking sheet, brushed side up. With about 6 or 7 minutes left for the mushrooms, put the bread into the oven alongside the mushrooms and toast until the bread is golden brown and crisp.

4. Meanwhile, fill a medium saucepan with plenty of water and bring to a boil over high heat. Once boiling, decrease the heat to medium-high and carefully break in the eggs. Poach for 1½ minutes for a runny yolk (or a little longer for a firmer set).

5. Divide the brioche among four plates and top each slice with the mushrooms so that they are all ready. Using a slotted spoon, remove the eggs from the water and spoon them on top of the mushrooms. Sprinkle each egg with a pinch of salt and a pinch of pepper flakes and serve warm, with a spoonful of sour cream alongside.

Scrambled harissa tofu

This was brought onto our menu as a vegan option for breakfast. It's been flying off the pass to all of our customers, vegan or not, ever since, as an alternative to eggs. We serve it on thick slices of grilled sourdough bread with a fresh green salad alongside. It's also lovely with a sprinkle of crispy fried shallots. If you think you'll get into the habit of making this for breakfast, double or quadruple the harissa onions—a batch keeps well in the fridge for around 5 days and turns this into a meal that can be ready in 5 minutes. Thanks to Claire Hodgson.

I. Place a large frying pan over medium-high heat and add the oil. Add the onions and fry for 9–10 minutes, stirring frequently, until caramelized and soft.

2. While the onions are frying, mix the cucumber, chiles, avocado, cilantro, oil, lime juice, and nigella seeds with a rounded ¼ tsp salt and set aside.

3. Add the harissa to the onions and continue to stir for 1 minute, then add the tofu and ¾ tsp salt. Use a potato masher to break up the tofu so it looks like scrambled egg and continue to heat for 2 minutes, until it's hot. Serve the scrambled tofu on the toast with the salad alongside.

Serves six

2 tbsp olive oil

2 onions, thinly sliced (3 cups/300g)

AVOCADO AND CUCUMBER SALAD

½ **English cucumber,** sliced in half lengthwise, seeded, and thinly sliced on an angle (¾ cup/180g)

2 green chiles, seeded and thinly sliced

3 ripe avocados, thinly sliced (14 oz/400g)

I cup/20g cilantro leaves

I tbsp olive oil

2 tbsp lime juice

I tsp nigella seeds

salt

1½ tbsp rose harissa (or 50 percent more or less, depending on variety; see page 301)

1½ lb/700g silken tofu, drained

6 slices of sourdough, toasted

Avocado butter on toast with tomato salsa

Serves two generously or four as a snack

2 or 3 very ripe avocados, at room temperature, flesh scooped out to get 9 oz/250g

¼ **cup/60g unsalted butter,** softened and cut into ¾-inch/2cm cubes

3 limes: finely zest to get 2 tsp, then juice to get 2 tbsp

salt

½ **cup/10g tarragon leaves,** roughly chopped

½ **cup/10g dill,** roughly chopped

7 oz/200g cherry tomatoes, quartered

2 tsp capers, finely chopped

2 tbsp olive oil, plus a little extra to serve

black pepper

4 slices of sourdough (10 oz/300g)

1 small garlic clove, peeled and halved

¼ **tsp cumin seeds,** toasted and crushed

The only way to make a creamy, rich avocado even more creamy and rich is, of course, to add some creamy rich butter. Don't worry that it will be a case of too much of a good thing; the salsa does what all good salsas do, bringing freshness, sharpness, and balance to whatever it sits alongside.

Make sure your avocados are nice and ripe and that your butter is supersoft so that they blend together properly. Don't be tempted to speed things along by melting the butter, which will cause it to separate. Just leave it at room temperature for a few hours. Both the salsa and avocado butter can be made 1 day in advance, if you like. Store them separately in the fridge.

1. Put the avocado and butter into the bowl of a small food processor with half the lime zest, half the lime juice, and ½ tsp salt. Blitz until smooth, scraping down the sides of the bowl a couple of times if you need to. Transfer to a small bowl along with two-thirds of the tarragon and dill. Fold in the herbs, then refrigerate for 10 minutes.

2. To make the salsa, mix together the tomatoes, capers, remaining lime zest, remaining lime juice and the oil with a good grind of pepper. Set aside until ready to serve.

3. Grill or toast the bread, then rub one side of each piece with the cut side of the garlic clove. Leave the bread to cool down just a little, then spread each slice with the avocado butter and top with the tomato salsa. Sprinkle with the cumin seeds and the remaining herbs. Finish with a grind of pepper and a drizzle of oil, and serve.

Beet, caraway, and goat cheese bread

Makes one loaf, ten slices

½ **cup/50g rolled oats**

½ **cup/20g thyme**
   leaves, finely chopped

⅓ **cup/50g pumpkin**
   seeds

2 tsp caraway seeds

2 tsp nigella seeds

¾ **cup/100g all-purpose**
   flour

⅔ **cup/100g plus 2 tbsp**
   whole wheat flour

2 tsp baking powder

¼ **tsp baking soda**

salt

1 medium beet, peeled
   and finely grated
   (2 cups/200g)

2 large eggs

⅓ **cup/80ml sunflower**
   oil, plus 1 tbsp extra
   for greasing

⅓ **cup/80g sour cream**

1 tbsp honey

¾ **oz/20g Parmesan,**
   finely grated

4¼ **oz/120g young and**
   creamy goat cheese,
   roughly broken into
   ¾-inch/2cm pieces

Making a bread that requires no yeast or kneading has got to be the definition of simple! The texture is more cakey as a result and best eaten with some salted butter (not used to make sandwiches). If you are warming it through, do so in the oven rather than in the toaster, as it's quite crumbly. Once baked, it will keep in an airtight container for 1 week or in the freezer for up to 1 month—thaw before slicing and toasting.

1. Preheat the oven to 400°F. Grease an 8 x 4-inch/20 x 10cm loaf pan and line with parchment paper.

2. Mix the oats, thyme, pumpkin, caraway, and nigella seeds in a small bowl. Put both flours into a separate bowl with the baking powder, baking soda, and ¾ tsp of salt. Whisk to combine and aerate, then add the grated beet and all but 1 tbsp of the oat and seed mix. Don't stir the mixture; just set it aside.

3. In a separate bowl, whisk the eggs, oil, sour cream, honey, and Parmesan. Pour over the flour and beet mixture, then, using a spatula, mix to combine. Add the goat cheese and carefully fold through, trying not to break the pieces as you go.

4. Spread the mixture evenly into the prepared loaf pan and sprinkle with the remaining 1 tbsp of the oat and seed mix. Bake for 40 minutes, then cover tightly with foil and bake for another 40 minutes. A skewer inserted into the middle will not come out completely clean, but it should not be too wet. Remove from the oven and let stand for 5 minutes, then turn out onto a wire rack and invert the bread so it is resting seed side up. The exterior will be quite crisp and dark. Cool for at least 20 minutes before slicing.

Cornbread with Cheddar, feta, and jalapeño

This is such a nice thing to bring to the table, served hot from the oven, out of the pan. It's a stand-alone bread—delicious as it is— but also happy to share a plate with bacon and avocado salad.

This bread is best eaten on the day it's baked, but it's still fine the next day; just warm it through in the oven. It also freezes well, for up to 1 month. If you don't have any fresh corn, you can defrost frozen corn kernels to use instead.

1. Heat the oven to 375°F.

2. Put a large (10-inch/25cm) ovenproof cast-iron pan over high heat. Once hot, add the corn and dry-fry for 4–5 minutes, stirring from time to time, until slightly blackened. Remove from the pan and set aside to cool.

3. Sift the flour, baking powder, baking soda, cumin, and cayenne into a large bowl. Add the sugar, along with 1 ½ tsp salt and a good grind of pepper. Stir and set aside.

4. Put the polenta, sour cream, eggs, and ½ cup/120ml of the oil into a separate bowl and whisk lightly. Add to the dry ingredients, then fold in the green onions, cilantro, jalapeño, and toasted corn until just combined.

5. Use the remaining 1 tbsp of oil to lightly grease the base and sides of the pan used to toast the corn, then pour in the cornbread mixture and scatter all the topping ingredients over it. Bake for 40–45 minutes, until a skewer comes out clean. Serve the cornbread hot, straight from the oven, or let cool for 30 minutes and serve warm or at room temperature the same day. If serving it the next day, warm it through in the oven just before you need it.

Serves ten to twelve

1 small ear corn, kernels cut off (mounded 1 cup/150g)

1 cup/140g all-purpose flour

1 tsp baking powder

½ tsp baking soda

1 tbsp ground cumin

1 tsp cayenne

firmly packed ¼ cup/ 50g light brown sugar

salt and black pepper

1⅓ cups/180g instant polenta

1½ cups/360g sour cream

2 large eggs

9 tbsp/135ml olive oil

4 green onions, roughly chopped

½ cup/10g cilantro leaves, chopped

1 jalapeño chile, finely chopped

FOR THE TOPPING

3½ oz/100g feta, crumbled

1¼ cups/100g aged Cheddar, coarsely grated

1 jalapeño chile, cut into thin rounds

½ red onion, cut into ¼-inch/½cm slices

2 tsp nigella seeds

Pea, za'atar, and feta fritters

Makes eight fritters,
to serve four to eight

1 lb 2 oz/500g frozen peas, defrosted

4¼ oz/120g ricotta

3 large eggs, beaten

1 lemon: finely zest to get 1 tsp, then cut it into 6 wedges, to serve

salt and black pepper

3 tbsp za'atar

⅔ cup/100g all-purpose flour

1½ tsp baking powder

1 cup/20g mint leaves, finely shredded

7 oz/200g feta, crumbled into ¾-inch/2cm pieces

about 3⅓ cups/800ml sunflower oil, for frying

This is pretty much a roll call of my favorite things: green peas, ricotta, za'atar, and feta. Add the words fritter *and* fried *and I'm the one at the stove, eating them straight from the pan, all hot and crispy. For those with more restraint, they also work at room temperature, though they lose their crunch. The batter can be made in advance and kept in the fridge for 1 day; just hold back on adding the baking powder and mint until you are ready to start frying.*

I've served them here with a wedge of lemon to squeeze on top, but if you want to add an extra twist, make a little sour cream sauce to have instead of (or as well as) the lemon. Just mix 1¼ cups/300g sour cream with ½ cup/10g chopped mint leaves, 2 tsp dried mint, ½ tsp finely grated lemon zest, and ¼ tsp salt.

1. Put the peas into a food processor and pulse a few times until roughly crushed, then transfer to a large bowl. Add the ricotta, eggs, lemon zest, ¾ tsp salt, and a good grind of pepper. Mix well, then add the za'atar, flour, and baking powder. Mix until just combined, then gently fold in the mint and feta; you don't want the chunks of feta to break up.

2. Pour the oil in a medium saucepan and place over medium-high heat. Once hot, use 2 small spoons to scoop up balls or quenelles of the mixture. Don't worry about making them uniform in shape, but they should be about 1½ inches/4cm wide. Carefully lower them into the oil—you should be able to do 4 at a time—and fry for 3–4 minutes, turning once, until cooked through and golden brown. If they are cooking too quickly and taking on too much color, just decrease the temperature so that the middle also cooks through. Using a slotted spoon, transfer to a paper towel–lined plate while you continue with the remaining fritters. Serve warm, with a wedge of lemon alongside.

Iranian herb fritters

Makes eight fritters, to serve four to eight (depending on whether everyone is having one in a pita or two as they are)

2 cups/40g dill, finely chopped

2 cups/40g basil leaves, finely chopped

2 cups/40g cilantro leaves, finely chopped

1½ tsp ground cumin

1 cup/50g fresh breadcrumbs (from about 2 slices, crusts left on if soft)

3 tbsp barberries (or currants, see page 299)

⅓ cup/25g walnut halves, lightly toasted and roughly chopped

8 large eggs, beaten

salt

¼ cup/60ml sunflower oil, for frying

These can be snacked on as they are, at room temperature, or served with a green tahini sauce and some extra herbs. If you want to make the tahini sauce, just blitz 3 tbsp/50g tahini, 1½ cups/30g parsley, ½ crushed garlic clove, 2 tbsp lemon juice, and ⅛ tsp salt for 30 seconds and pour in ½ cup/120ml water. Adding the water last allows the parsley to get really broken up and turns the sauce as green as can be. This sauce is lovely spooned over all sorts of things—grilled meat and fish and roasted vegetables, for example—so double or triple the batch and keep it in the fridge. It keeps well for about 5 days. You might want to thin it with a little water or lemon juice to get it back to the right consistency.

These fritters are a bit of a fridge-raid, using up whatever herbs you have around. As long as you keep the total net weight the same and use a mixture of herbs, this will still work wonderfully. The batter will keep, uncooked, for 1 day in the fridge.

Alternatively, pile the fritters into pita bread with condiments, such as a combination of yogurt, chile sauce, pickled vegetables, and tahini. You'd just need one fritter per person, rather than two.

1. Place all the ingredients, apart from the oil, in a large bowl with ½ tsp of salt. Mix well to combine and set aside.

2. Put 2 tbsp of the oil into a large nonstick pan and place over medium-high heat. Once hot, add ladles of batter to the pan. Do 4 fritters at a time, if you can—you want each of them to be about 5 inches/12cm wide—otherwise just do 2 or 3 at a time. Fry for 1–2 minutes on each side, until crisp and golden brown. Transfer to a paper towel–lined plate and set aside while you continue with the remaining batter and oil.

3. Serve warm or at room temperature.

Raw Veg

Chilled cucumber, cauliflower, and ginger soup

Serves four

4 fresh mint sprigs

5-inch/12cm piece of ginger, peeled (3¼ oz/90g); two-thirds roughly grated and the remaining third cut into thin slices, about ⅛-inch/3mm thick

salt

½ large cauliflower, broken up into ¾-inch/2cm florets (3½ cups/350g)

3 large English cucumbers (or 8 small Lebanese cucumbers), peeled, seeded (if large), and roughly chopped (4 cups/650g)

1 garlic clove, crushed

2 cups plus 2 tbsp/500g Greek-style yogurt

2 tbsp lemon juice

white pepper

¼ cup/60ml olive oil

⅔ cup/70g sliced almonds

2 tsp dried mint

Gazpacho is so often the go-to for a chilled summer soup that it's easy to forget about other options. This alternative is fresh and full of textures. If you see Lebanese cucumbers, do get them. They're smaller and firmer than the larger cucumbers, and because they have so much less water, have a lot more taste.

This soup will keep for 2 days in the fridge. The almonds need to be fried and added just before serving.

1. Pour 3⅓ cups/800ml of water into a medium saucepan and add the fresh mint sprigs, the thinly sliced ginger, and 2 tsp salt. Bring to a boil, then add the cauliflower and blanch for 2–3 minutes, until just cooked but still al dente. Drain and set aside. Discard the mint and ginger.

2. Place the cucumbers in an upright blender or food processor with the grated ginger, garlic, yogurt, lemon juice, 1 tsp salt, and ½ tsp white pepper. Blitz until smooth, then chill in the fridge for at least 1 hour.

3. Heat the oil in a small skillet over medium heat and add the almonds. Cook for 3–4 minutes, stirring often, until the almonds are a light golden brown. Transfer to a separate bowl and stir in the dried mint. Add a pinch of salt and set aside to cool.

4. When ready to serve, divide the cauliflower florets among four bowls and pour the chilled soup over them. Spoon the almond mix on top and serve.

Beefsteak tomato carpaccio with green onion and ginger salsa

As ever with tomato dishes, particularly when the tomatoes are uncooked, this is all about the quality of the ingredients. The tomatoes need to be superripe and sweet and the sherry vinegar needs to be best quality (such as Valdespino). Double or triple the salsa, if you like; it's absolutely delicious spooned over all sorts of things—roast chicken, for example—or on toast topped with mozzarella or avocado (or both), and it will keep in the fridge for up to 5 days. Once assembled, this dish will also keep in the fridge for up to 6 hours, but bring it back to room temperature before serving. Thanks to Ixta Belfrage for spotting this on the table next to her in Chinatown and being intrigued enough to ask for a plate.

Serves four as a side

1¼-inch/3cm piece of ginger, peeled and roughly chopped (1 tbsp)

flaked sea salt

4 green onions, very thinly sliced (¾ cup/45g)

2½ tbsp sunflower oil (or other mild oil)

2 tsp good-quality sherry vinegar

14 oz/400g beefsteak tomatoes (about 2, depending on size), sliced ¹⁄₁₆-inch/2mm thick

¼ green chile, seeded and finely chopped

1½ tbsp finely shredded cilantro

1 tbsp olive oil

1. Put the ginger and ½ tsp flaked salt into a pestle and mortar and crush to a fine paste. Transfer to a bowl with the green onions and stir to combine.

2. Put the oil in a small pan and place over low heat until just warm (you don't want it to heat too much). Pour over the green onions and add 1 tsp of the vinegar. Stir and set aside.

3. Lay the tomatoes on a large platter, with the slices slightly overlapping. Season with ¼ tsp of flaked salt and drizzle with the remaining 1 tsp of vinegar. Spoon the green onion and ginger salsa evenly over the tomatoes (or use your hands to better effect), scatter the chile and cilantro on top and finish with the olive oil.

Tomato and cucumber raita

The chile paste will keep for 3 days in a sealed container in the fridge. Once assembled, the dish will keep in the fridge for up to 2 days.

Serves four generously

GREEN CHILE PASTE

1½ **small preserved lemons,** seeds discarded, skin and flesh roughly chopped (¼ cup/50g)

2 **green chiles,** seeded and chopped

2 **garlic cloves,** passed through a garlic press

2½ **tbsp olive oil**

⅔ **cup/200g Greek-style yogurt**

½ **cup/10g mint leaves,** finely shredded

1 **tbsp lemon juice**

2 **tsp cumin seeds,** toasted and finely crushed

1 **English cucumber** (or 3 or 4 small Lebanese cucumbers), quartered lengthwise, seeded, and flesh cut into ½-inch/1cm dice (2 cups/300g)

½ **onion,** finely chopped (½ cup/75g)

7 oz/200g **cherry tomatoes,** quartered

salt

1. Place all the ingredients for the chile paste in the bowl of a food processor, with ¼ tsp of salt. Blitz to form a rough paste and set aside.

2. Put the yogurt in a bowl and whisk with the mint, lemon juice, 1½ tsp of the cumin seeds, and rounded ¼ tsp salt. Add the cucumber, onion, and tomatoes and stir gently. Transfer to a shallow bowl and top with chile paste. Swirl lightly, sprinkle with the remaining ½ tsp of cumin seeds and serve.

Zucchini, thyme, and walnut salad

The garlic oil can be made in advance and kept for 3 days at room temperature. Zucchini become watery soon after the salt has been added, so if preparing these more than 4–6 hours in advance, hold back on the seasoning and lemon juice until just before serving.

Serves four

3 tbsp olive oil

6 thyme sprigs

1 lemon: finely shave the peel to get about 6 strips, then juice to get 2 tbsp

1 garlic clove, skin on and smashed with the flat side of a knife

4 zucchini (a mix of green and yellow looks great if you can find both), sliced into long thin ribbons using a potato peeler or mandoline (1 lb 5 oz/600g)

⅔ cup/60g walnut halves, roughly chopped

salt and black pepper

¾ cup/15g basil, roughly shredded

1. Put the oil, thyme, lemon strips, and garlic into a small skillet. Place over low heat to warm and infuse for 8 minutes, until the oil becomes aromatic and the garlic, lemon, and thyme start to color. Remove from the heat and let cool. Once cool enough to handle, strain the oil into a large bowl. Remove the thyme leaves from the sprigs and add to the oil. Discard the lemon and garlic.

2. Add the zucchini, walnuts, lemon juice, a rounded ¼ tsp salt, and pepper to the oil. Massage all the ingredients for a minute—the zucchini will break up slightly—add the basil, and serve.

Tomato and bread salad with anchovies and capers

Get as big a range of tomatoes as you can here. A clash of color looks just great. I could eat this every day through the summer just as it is or with a thin tuna steak alongside.

The toasted sourdough will keep for 4 hours and the tomatoes will keep in the fridge for up to 6 hours—but hold back on adding the basil until just before serving. Keep everything separate, bring back to room temperature, and assemble when ready to serve.

1. Put the garlic, anchovy, and olive oil in a medium saucepan, along with ½ tsp flaked salt, and place over low heat. Cook gently for 10 minutes, stirring occasionally, until the garlic and anchovies soften when mashed with the back of a spoon. Make sure not to heat the oil too much or the garlic will burn; if the oil does start to bubble, just remove the pan from the heat until it cools. After 10 minutes, remove the pan from the heat and add the sourdough chunks to the hot oil. Toss the bread until well coated, then transfer the bread to a large bowl. Leave the anchovy and garlic oil in the pan.

2. Mix the tomatoes, lemon zest, lemon juice, capers, parsley, and basil in a separate bowl.

3. When ready to serve, add the tomato mixture to the bowl of bread. Carefully toss everything, then transfer to a platter or serving dish. Drizzle with the remaining anchovy and garlic oil and finish with the chile flakes.

Serves four to six

4 garlic cloves, crushed

6 anchovy fillets in oil, drained and finely chopped (about 1 tbsp)

7½ tbsp/110ml olive oil

flaked sea salt

3½ oz/100g sourdough, crusts left on, sliced ¾ inch/2cm thick, lightly toasted, then cut into 1½-inch/4cm chunks

1 lb 2 oz/500g ripe tomatoes, cut into 1½-inch/4cm chunks

1 lemon: finely zest to get 1 tsp, then juice to get 2 tsp

1 tbsp capers, roughly chopped

¼ cup/5g parsley leaves, finely chopped

¼ cup/5g basil leaves, finely chopped, plus a few extra leaves to serve

1 tsp Urfa chile flakes (or ½ tsp of other crushed red pepper flakes)

Tomatoes with sumac shallots and pine nuts

Serves four

I large shallot, sliced
   paper-thin (⅓ cup/70g)

I ½ tbsp sumac

**2 tsp white wine
   vinegar**

salt

**I ½ lb/700g mixed
   tomatoes** (a mix of
   large tiger, green and
   red plum, red and
   yellow cherry; or a
   single variety if that
   is all you can get)

2 tbsp olive oil

¾ cup/15g basil leaves

black pepper

¼ cup/25g pine nuts,
   toasted

The quality of your tomatoes makes all the difference here. They need to be the ripest and sweetest you can find. This is my go-to salad in the summer, eaten as is, with some crusty bread to mop up the juices, or served as part of whatever else is on the table. Chunks of ripe avocado are also a nice addition.

The shallot slices can be prepared I day in advance and kept in the fridge. If you want to make the dish ahead, slice the tomatoes up to 6 hours in advance and store in the fridge, ready for the oil, basil, and seasoning to be added when you are ready to serve.

I. Place the shallot in a small bowl with the sumac, vinegar, and ⅛ tsp salt. Use your hands to mix them—you want the sumac to really be massaged into the shallots—then set aside for 30 minutes to soften.

2. Slice the large tomatoes in half lengthwise and then into ½-inch/1cm wedges and place in a large bowl. Slice the cherry tomatoes in half lengthwise and add to the bowl. Pour in the olive oil and mix gently with the basil leaves, a rounded ¼ tsp salt, and a generous grind of pepper.

3. Arrange the tomatoes on a large platter. Spread the shallot slices over them, lifting some of the tomatoes and basil from under the shallots to rest on top. Sprinkle with the pine nuts and serve.

Pictured right with Chopped salad with tahini and za'atar (page 36)

Chopped salad with tahini and za'atar

*Serves four as a starter
or side*

6 ripe plum tomatoes
(or any other sweet
red tomato), cut into
½-inch/1cm dice
(4 cups/650g)

**3 or 4 Lebanese (small)
cucumbers** (or
1 English cucumber),
cut into ½-inch/1cm
dice (2 cups/300g)

1 red bell pepper,
seeded and cut into
½-inch/1cm dice
(1 cup/150g)

5 green onions, thinly
sliced on an angle
(rounded ¾ cup/50g)

¾ cup/15g cilantro,
roughly chopped

2 tbsp lemon juice

3 tbsp olive oil

salt

7 oz/200g feta, cut into
4 rectangular blocks
(optional)

¼ cup/70g tahini

2 tsp za'atar

Adding tahini to an otherwise familiar tomato and cucumber salad can be a real revelation. You need to start with a brand of tahini that is creamy, nutty, and smooth enough to pour. These tend to be the Israeli, Palestinian, or Lebanese brands (rather than the Greek and Cypriot ones, which don't taste as good). This is lovely as a starter, with the blocks of feta, or served alongside some grilled lamb or rice with lentils (with or without the feta).

1. Place the tomatoes in a sieve sitting over a bowl. Set aside for 20 minutes to allow some of the liquid to drain away. Place the tomatoes in a large bowl (discard the drained liquid), then add the cucumbers, red pepper, green onions, cilantro, lemon juice, oil, and ½ tsp salt. Mix to combine.

2. When you are ready to serve, transfer the salad to a serving bowl, add the feta, and mix gently. Pour the tahini on top and finish with the za'atar and a final sprinkle of salt.

Pictured on page 35

Gem lettuce with fridge-raid dressing

Serves four as a side

½ **very ripe avocado,** flesh scooped out (3¼ oz/90g)

1½-**inch/4cm piece of ginger,** peeled and roughly chopped (2 tbsp)

1 **small garlic clove,** crushed

2 **lemons:** finely zest 1 to get 1 tsp, then juice both to get 3 tbsp

1 **green chile,** roughly chopped

1 **tbsp tahini**

5 **tbsp plus 2 tsp/ 85ml olive oil**

salt

½ **cup/10g basil leaves**

½ **cup/10g tarragon leaves**

½ **cup/10g dill**

½ **cup/10g parsley leaves**

½ **cup/10g cilantro leaves**

¼ **cup/60ml water**

4 **gem lettuces,** trimmed at the bottom and cut lengthwise into eighths (14 oz/400g)

2 **tsp black sesame seeds** (or white), lightly toasted

This started off as a clean-up of all the herbs Tara had lying around in her fridge that needed using up (but it was so good she ended up buying the herbs all over again to keep making it).

If you're doing the same, clearing out the vegetable drawer, don't be too precious about the weight of individual herbs: so long as you keep the total net weight about the same, you'll be fine.

Make double the recipe for the dressing if you like. It keeps for 3 days in the fridge and is lovely spooned over all sorts of things: a chicken salad or tuna Niçoise, for example, or roasted root vegetables or a simple tomato and feta salad.

Get ahead if you like by making the dressing up to 3 days in advance and storing in the fridge.

1. Put the avocado, ginger, garlic, lemon zest, lemon juice, chile, and tahini into the bowl of a food processor with 5 tbsp/75ml of the oil and a rounded ¼ tsp salt. Blitz to a smooth paste, then add the basil, tarragon, dill, parsley, and cilantro. Blitz again, then, with the machine still running, slowly pour in the water until smooth and combined.

2. Mix the gem lettuce with the remaining 2 tsp of oil and ⅛ tsp salt until combined. Transfer to a platter, spoon the dressing on top, and sprinkle with the sesame seeds.

Cucumber and lamb's lettuce salad

Serves four

DRESSING

1 tbsp lemon juice

1 small garlic clove, minced

1¼-inch/3cm piece of ginger, finely grated (1 tbsp)

rounded 1 tbsp plain yogurt

flaked sea salt

5 baby cucumbers (or 1½ English cucumbers; 1 lb 2 oz/500g)

1½ cups/30g lamb's lettuce

½ cup/10g mint leaves

½ cup/10g cilantro leaves

1 tsp nigella seeds

It can be easy to get a bit set in your ways with salad dressing. Trying something new—as I do here, with the ginger and yogurt—can be a real joy. Prep the cucumbers in advance if you like, but don't mix them with the dressing until just before serving; the salt in the dressing releases the water in the cucumber, so it will become watery if it sits around for too long. If you start with regular-size cucumbers that's fine, but you'll need to cut out the watery core before slicing. This is absolutely lovely with all sorts of things—a roast leg of lamb, some grilled salmon, or the pea, za'atar, and feta fritters, on page 20, to mention just three.

The dressing can be made 2 days in advance and kept in the fridge. Slice and refrigerate the cucumbers up to 6 hours in advance.

1. For the dressing, whisk lemon juice, garlic, ginger, and yogurt with a rounded ¼ tsp flaked salt and set aside.

2. Take each cucumber and quarter lengthwise. Then cut each long quarter diagonally into ¼-inch/½cm slices and place in a large bowl with the lamb's lettuce, mint, and cilantro. Gently mix the cucumber and leaves with the dressing and spread in a large shallow bowl. Sprinkle with the nigella seeds and serve.

Pictured right with 5-spice peach and raspberry salad (page 41)

Watermelon, green apple, and lime salad

This is delicious as it is—it screams summer, it screams virtuous and it definitely screams delicious—but some roasted peanuts, pistachios, or cashews sprinkled on top also work as a nice addition.

Serves six as a side

½ **medium watermelon** (2¾ lb/1.3kg), rind and seeds discarded and flesh cut into 2¾-inch/ 7cm-long, ¼-inch/ ½cm-wide batons (4¾ cups/600g)

2 **Granny Smith apples,** cored and cut into 2¾-inch/7cm-long, ¼-inch/½cm-wide batons (2 cups/250g)

3 **limes:** finely zest to get 2 tsp, then juice to get 3 tbsp

1 **tbsp olive oil**

1 **lemongrass stalk,** trimmed, woody outer leaves discarded, then finely chopped (2 tbsp)

¼ **cup/5g mint leaves**

½ **cup/10g cilantro leaves**

flaked sea salt

1½ **tsp black mustard seeds,** lightly toasted

1. Mix the salad just before you're ready to serve, otherwise it will get too soggy. In a large bowl, combine the watermelon, apples, lime zest, lime juice, olive oil, and lemongrass with three-quarters of the herbs and ¾ tsp of flaked salt. Using your hands as a natural sieve, arrange the salad on a platter. There will be quite a bit of juice at the bottom of the bowl; you don't need it. Scatter with the remaining herbs, sprinkle with the mustard seeds and ¼ tsp of flaked salt, and serve.

Pictured above right

5-spice peach and raspberry salad

You don't want this salad to be too sweet, so for the best results start with peaches that are not too ripe. This looks so perfectly summery and also works really well at a barbecue, where the fruit complements and cuts through all sorts of meat. Some slow-cooked pork belly alongside is a particularly winning combination.

Serves four as a side

1 ½ **tbsp cider vinegar**

1 **tsp maple syrup**

¼ **tsp Chinese 5-spice powder**

1 **tbsp olive oil**

1 **shallot,** thinly sliced (¼ cup/20g)

salt

3 ½ **oz/100g raspberries**

3 **firm peaches,** halved, pits removed, cut into ¼-inch/½cm wedges (2 cups/290g)

2 **cups/40g watercress**

¼ **head radicchio,** cut into ¾-inch/2cm slices (2 cups/50g)

1. In a large bowl, mix together the vinegar, maple syrup, 5-spice powder, oil, and shallot with a rounded ¼ tsp salt. Add the raspberries, lightly crushing them with the back of a fork, then add the peaches, watercress, and radicchio. Mix well and serve.

Burrata with grilled grapes and basil

Burrata—which means "buttered" in Italian—is one of life's great pleasures. The outside is firm mozzarella, the inside an oozy combination of stracciatella and cream. The combination of the three is unsurprisingly good. Burrata can be paired with all sorts of flavors— citrus fruit or juice, sweet balsamic, peppery arugula, or toasted spices. Here, sweet red grapes are skewered and grilled—a method that is as simple as it is impressive. If you want to get ahead, marinate the grapes in the fridge for up to 1 day before grilling. If you can't get hold of burrata, balls of buffalo mozzarella make an absolutely fine alternative.

1. Put the grapes in a medium bowl with the vinegar, oil, garlic, sugar, 1 tsp of the fennel seeds, ¼ tsp of flaked salt, and plenty of pepper. Mix well and marinate for at least 1 hour and up to 1 day. Thread 5 or 6 grapes onto each skewer. Don't throw away the marinade; you'll need it when serving.

2. Place a grill pan over high heat and ventilate your kitchen well. Once hot, add the grape skewers in batches and grill for 2–3 minutes, turning after 1½ minutes. Remove from the heat.

3. When ready to serve, tear the balls of burrata in half and place one-half on each plate. Arrange the grape skewers to lean against them—2 per portion—and spoon 1½ tsp of the marinade over the cheese. Alternatively, arrange on a platter to serve a crowd. Sprinkle with the remaining ½ tsp of fennel seeds, garnish with a sprig of basil, and serve.

Serves six as a generous starter

11¼ oz/320g seedless red grapes, pulled off their vine

2 tbsp Valdespino vinegar (or other best-quality sherry vinegar)

3 tbsp olive oil

1 garlic clove, crushed

1½ tsp dark brown sugar

1½ tsp fennel seeds, toasted and lightly crushed

flaked sea salt and black pepper

3 large balls of burrata or buffalo mozzarella (1 lb 5 oz/600g)

6 small purple or green basil sprigs (¼ cup/5g), to serve

Cauliflower "tabbouleh"

Serves six

1 large cauliflower
   (1¾ lb/800g)

**5 tbsp/75ml lemon
   juice,** from 3 lemons

salt

7 green onions,
   finely chopped
   (scant 1 cup/70g)

2½ cups/50g parsley,
   roughly chopped

1¼ cups/25g dill,
   roughly chopped

1 cup/20g mint,
   roughly chopped

1 tsp ground allspice

3 tbsp olive oil

black pepper

**⅔ cup/100g
   pomegranate seeds**
   (from ½ pomegranate)

If you're doubling or tripling this recipe, break the cauliflower into florets and pop them into a food processor (rather than grating by hand). Pulse a few times to blitz it up into tabbouleh-like pieces, but don't overwork the machine, as the cauliflower will turn to a mush. Toasted pistachios, roughly chopped, can be used instead of (or as well as) the pomegranate seeds, if you want a crunchy garnish.

1. Hold the cauliflower by its stalk and grate the florets and smaller stalks coarsely, on the large holes of a box grater. (Alternatively, you can use a food processor with its largest grating attachment in place, which is quicker.) Once grated, the cauliflower looks like cooked bulgur wheat and should weigh about 1½ lb/700g. The cauliflower stalk can be sliced thinly and added to salads.

2. Place the grated cauliflower in a large bowl along with the lemon juice and 1¼ tsp salt. Set aside to marinate for 20 minutes, then add the green onions, parsley, dill, mint, allspice, oil, and a generous grind of black pepper. Gently mix to combine, transfer to a serving plate or bowl, sprinkle with the pomegranate seeds, and serve.

Green onion and herb salad

This is lovely alongside all sorts of meat: it's as green- and herb-filled as a spring roast chicken wants (page 227) and as citrusy and refreshing as any slow-cooked lamb (page 215) or beef meatballs (page 220) might demand.

If you can get hold of baby cucumbers for this, then do; they have a lot less water in them than the standard ones. If you start with the large ones that's fine, but slice in half lengthwise, scoop out the watery seeded core, and proceed.

The dressing can be made the day before. Prepare the salad to the point of adding the herbs and salt up to 4–6 hours in advance.

1. To make the dressing, place the ginger in a pestle and mortar and crush to form a rough paste. Mix with the lemon juice, oil, and salt and set aside.

2. Place the green onions, cucumbers, bell pepper, mint, and cilantro in a large bowl. Add the dressing, and toss well. Add the nigella seeds and salt to taste, toss again, and serve.

Serves six as a side

DRESSING

1½-inch/4cm piece of
  ginger, peeled and finely
  chopped (¼ cup/25g)

2 tbsp lemon juice

2½ tbsp olive oil

¼ **tsp salt**

15 green onions, cut
  into quarters lengthwise
  and finely chopped
  (2¼ cups/150g)

**2 small Lebanese
  cucumbers** (or ½ small
  English cucumber),
  unpeeled and cut
  into ½-inch/1cm dice
  (1 cup/150g)

1 green bell pepper,
  cut in half lengthwise,
  seeded, and cut into
  ½-inch/1cm dice
  (1 cup/150g)

¾ **cup/15g mint leaves,**
  finely shredded

¾ **cup/15g cilantro,**
  roughly chopped

½ **tsp nigella seeds**

salt

Cooked Veg

Curried lentil, tomato, and coconut soup

Serves four

2 tbsp coconut oil
or sunflower oil

1 onion, finely chopped
(1¼ cups/160g)

**1 tbsp medium curry
powder**

**¼ tsp crushed red
pepper flakes**

2 garlic cloves, crushed

**2-inch/5cm piece
of ginger,** peeled
and finely chopped
(rounded ¼ cup/30g)

¾ cup/150g red lentils,
rinsed and drained

**1 (14.5 oz/400g) can
chopped tomatoes**

**1¼ cups/25g cilantro
stems,** roughly
chopped, plus ¼ cup/5g
leaves, to garnish

2½ cups/600ml water

salt and black pepper

**1 (13.5oz/400ml) can
coconut milk**

I like the rough texture of this soup—with the lentils still holding their shape and the cilantro distinct—but you can also blitz it before serving, if you prefer things smooth. This soup can be made 4 days in advance if kept in the fridge, and up to 1 month if frozen.

Cilantro stems can all too often be thrown away, but they shouldn't be—they have the texture of chives and taste, unsurprisingly, of cilantro. Serve this soup with lime wedges, if you like, for a citrusy kick.

1. Put the oil into a medium saucepan and place over medium-high heat. Add the onion and fry for 8 minutes, stirring frequently, until soft and caramelized. Add the curry powder, pepper flakes, garlic, and ginger and continue to fry for 2 minutes, stirring continuously. Add the lentils, stir through for 1 minute, then add the tomatoes, cilantro stems, water, 1 tsp of salt, and a very generous grind of pepper.

2. Pour the coconut milk into a bowl and gently whisk until smooth and creamy. Set aside ¼ cup/60ml—you'll need this when serving—and add all the remaining coconut milk to the soup. Bring to a boil, then decrease the heat to medium and simmer gently for 25 minutes, until the lentils are soft but still holding their shape. Add a little bit more water—about 7–10 tbsp/ 100–150ml—if your soup needs thinning.

3. Divide the soup among four bowls, drizzle with the reserved coconut milk, sprinkle with cilantro leaves, and serve.

Pictured on page 51, bottom

Zucchini, pea, and basil soup

A slightly heartier version of this soup—made with chicken stock and topped with pan-fried cubes of ham or pancetta—is also delicious.

The key to keeping a green soup as green and vibrant as can be is not to overcook it. Once the peas and basil have been added to the pan you want to remove it from the heat and blitz it straightaway. This can be made 3 days in advance if kept in the fridge, and up to 1 month if frozen.

1. Put the oil into an extra-large saucepan and place over medium-high heat. Add the whole garlic cloves and fry for 2–3 minutes, stirring frequently, until they turn golden. Add the zucchini, 2 tsp of salt, and plenty of pepper and continue to fry for 3 minutes, stirring continuously, until starting to brown. Pour in the stock, along with the water, and bring to a boil over high heat. Cook for 7 minutes, until the zucchini are soft but still bright green.

2. Add the peas, stir through for 1 minute, then add the basil. Remove from the heat and, using an immersion blender, blitz until the soup is smooth and vibrant green.

3. When ready to serve, spoon into eight bowls and top with the feta and lemon zest. Finish with a good grind of black pepper and a drizzle of oil.

Serves eight

5 tbsp/75ml olive oil, plus extra to serve

1 head of garlic, cloves separated and peeled

about 6 zucchini, chopped into 1¼ inch/3cm-thick slices (9 cups/1.3kg)

salt and black pepper

1 qt/1L vegetable stock

2 cups/500ml water

4¼ cups/500g frozen peas

2½ cups/50g basil leaves

7 oz/200g feta, broken into ½–¾ inch/1–2cm pieces

1 lemon, finely zested to get 1 tsp

Pictured on page 51, top

Pumpkin, saffron, and orange soup

When they're in season, through autumn and winter, there are all sorts of weird and wonderful pumpkins and squash at the market. Winter squash are best for this soup—their consistency is firm and their flavor has a depth that is similar to sweet potatoes. You can also make it with summer squash (of which pumpkin is one)—the flesh will just be a bit more fibrous and watery.

The soup will keep in the fridge for 3 days, or can be frozen for up to 1 month, and the pumpkin seeds will keep well in a dry, sealed container for a good week. Double or triple the recipe for the pumpkin seeds— they are lovely to have around to sprinkle over other soups, salads, or roasted vegetables.

Serves four to six

**TOASTED
PUMPKIN SEEDS**
mounded ½ cup/80g
   pumpkin seeds
2 tsp maple syrup
¼ **tsp crushed red**
   pepper flakes

¼ **cup/60ml olive oil**
2 onions, sliced into
   1¼-inch/3cm wedges
   (3½ cups/350g)
**2½ lb/1.2kg pumpkin or
butternut squash,** peeled
and seeds removed, flesh
cut into 1¼-inch/3cm
cubes (8 cups/1kg)

salt and black pepper
1 qt/1L vegetable stock
2 tbsp rose harissa
   (or 50 percent more
   or less, depending on
   variety; see page 301)
¼ **tsp saffron threads**
1 orange, finely zested
   to get 1 tsp
¾ **cup/180g crème fraîche**
¼ **cup/5g cilantro leaves**

1. Preheat the oven to 375°F.

2. Mix everything for the pumpkin seeds in a small bowl, along with ¼ tsp salt. Spread onto a small parchment-lined baking sheet and toast for 15 minutes, until the seeds have popped and are starting to brown. Set aside to cool and then break up any clumps into bite-size pieces.

3. Increase the oven to 450°F.

4. Combine the oil, onions, and pumpkin in a large bowl with ¾ tsp salt and a good grind of pepper. Mix well and transfer to a large parchment-lined baking sheet. Roast for 25 minutes, until everything is soft and caramelized. Remove from the oven and set aside.

5. Put the stock into a stockpot with the harissa, saffron, orange zest, ½ tsp salt, and a good grind of pepper. Bring to a boil over high heat and, once boiling, carefully tip in the roasted pumpkin and onions, along with any oil from the sheet pan, into the stockpot. Stir through, then decrease the heat to medium and simmer for 5 minutes. Remove from the heat, stir in the crème fraîche, then, using an immersion blender (or transfer to a countertop blender if that's what you have), blitz until completely smooth.

6. Serve each portion with a sprinkle of toasted pumpkin seeds and cilantro.

Pictured on page 50

Steamed zucchini with garlic and oregano

Serves four as a starter or
part of a mezze plate

1¾ lb/800g mixed
   young zucchini
1 cup plus 1 tbsp/
   250ml chicken or
   vegetable stock
4 garlic cloves, sliced
   paper-thin
20 oregano sprigs
   (3 oz/20g)
flaked sea salt
2 tbsp olive oil

*Try to get small and young zucchini for this if you can—their
tenderness is heaven when steamed. I love the thin slices of raw garlic,
but if this doesn't appeal then just add the fried oregano leaves.*

*These are either a simple and delicate starter or work well served
alongside other mezze with some bread.*

1. Preheat the oven to 425°F.

2. If the zucchini are really small you can keep them whole, but,
for any larger ones, cut them into quarters, lengthwise, and sit
them in a high-sided ceramic baking dish, about 11 x 9 inches/27 x
22cm, cut side facing up. They should all be sitting together snugly.

3. Pour the stock into a small saucepan with half the garlic and
half the oregano sprigs. Bring to a boil. Sprinkle the zucchini
with ¾ tsp of flaked salt and then pour the boiling stock over
them. Cover the dish tightly with foil and bake for 45 minutes,
until the zucchini are completely soft. Remove from the oven
and set aside to slightly cool.

4. Remove the leaves from the remaining oregano sprigs and
discard the stems. Put the olive oil into a small frying pan and place
over medium-high heat. Once hot, add the leaves and fry for about
1½ minutes, until they begin to crisp up. Remove from the heat
and transfer to a small bowl.

5. When you are ready to serve, lift the zucchini out of the warm
stock and divide them among individual plates or arrange on one
platter. Drizzle with the oregano oil and crispy leaves, along with
½ tsp flaked salt. Sprinkle with the remaining garlic slices and serve.

Pictured on page 58

Crushed zucchini

This is lovely either as it is (or with a spoonful of yogurt), as part of a mezze spread, or served alongside some lamb or chicken. If you can get hold of the pale, slightly pear-shaped zucchini (widely available in Middle Eastern grocers), then do—their skin is soft, so they're easier to crush and bite through.

This dish can be made up to 1 day in advance, up to the point of the herbs and lemon being added. Keep in the fridge and add the herbs and lemon just before serving.

1. Preheat the oven to 425°F.

2. Place the zucchini in a bowl with the dried mint, thyme, oil, ¾ tsp of salt, and some black pepper. Mix, then transfer to a medium baking dish; the zucchini should form a single layer, cut side up and sitting slightly overlapping. Bake for 15 minutes, then add the garlic cloves and bake for another 15 minutes, until the zucchini have softened and taken on some color. Transfer everything to a colander (set over a bowl or the sink), pressing the zucchini so that they start to release some of their liquid. Set aside to cool for at least 30 minutes, discarding the liquid released.

3. Transfer the contents of the colander to a mixing bowl and squeeze the garlic cloves out of their skins (which can then be discarded). Mash everything together with a fork—if the skin of the zucchini is still a little tough, just use a knife to roughly chop them. Stir in the mint leaves, dill, and lemon juice and serve.

Serves four as a starter, side, or part of a mezze plate

3 large zucchini, cut in half lengthwise, then into 2½-inch/6cm pieces (4½ cups/850g)

1 tsp dried mint

¼ **cup/5g thyme leaves**

5 tbsp/70ml olive oil

salt and black pepper

1 head of garlic, cloves separated and unpeeled

2 tbsp chopped mint leaves

1½ **tbsp chopped dill**

1 tbsp lemon juice

Pictured on page 59

Stuffed zucchini with pine nut salsa

Stuffed vegetables would definitely be part of my last meal—I love them! Traditionally, stuffing vegetables has always been a bit of a labor of love but, here, a lot of labor has been removed without cost to the love. Try to get large zucchini, if you can—you'll be able to scrape them more easily without damaging them and have plenty of flesh to stuff back inside. A mix of yellow and green zucchini also looks great, if you can get hold of both.

You can make the stuffing a day ahead so that the zucchini are ready to be stuffed and grilled.

Serves two as a main or four as a side

2 large zucchini, halved lengthwise (1 lb 2 oz/500g)

½ **garlic clove,** minced

1 large egg, beaten

1½ **oz/40g Parmesan** (or pecorino), finely grated

scant 1 cup/40g fresh sourdough breadcrumbs (from about 1 slice, crust left on if soft)

salt

3½ **oz/100g cherry tomatoes,** quartered

1 large lemon: finely zest to get 2 tsp, then juice to get 1 tbsp

¼ **cup/5g finely chopped oregano leaves,** plus a few extra leaves to serve

mounded ¼ cup/ 35g pine nuts, lightly toasted

3 tbsp olive oil

1. Preheat the oven to 475°F.

2. Use a small spoon to hollow out the flesh of the zucchini and make them into the shape of canoes. Don't scrape them out completely, though—you want the sides to be about ½ inch/1cm thick and the zucchini should still hold their shape. Transfer the flesh to a sieve and squeeze and discard as much liquid as you can—you should be left with about 1 cup/100g of drained zucchini flesh. Put this into a medium bowl and stir in the garlic, egg, Parmesan, breadcrumbs, and ¼ tsp of salt. Use your hands to crush the tomatoes well, then add these to the bowl of zucchini mixture. Stir to combine and set aside.

3. In a separate bowl, mix the lemon zest, oregano, and pine nuts. Stir half of this into the zucchini mixture and set the rest aside for the salsa.

4. Place the hollowed zucchini on a medium baking sheet or ovenproof dish, hollowed side facing up. Drizzle 1 tbsp of oil (in total) over the zucchini and season with ⅛ tsp of salt (in total). Spoon the zucchini mixture back into the hollows and bake for 15 minutes, until the filling is set and golden brown.

5. While the zucchini are baking, make the salsa. Add the lemon juice, remaining 2 tbsp of oil, and ⅛ tsp of salt to the bowl of oregano and pine nuts. Let the zucchini cool a little. Spoon the salsa on top, sprinkle with oregano leaves, and serve.

Herby zucchini and peas with semolina porridge

The semolina porridge is a super-comforting base to all sorts of toppings. It works very well, for example, topped with a very simple beef ragout.

1. Put the butter into a large sauté pan with a lid and place over medium-high heat. Once the butter has melted, add the garlic and fry for 1–2 minutes, until starting to brown. Add the zucchini, ¾ tsp salt, and a good grind of pepper and cook for 5 minutes, stirring frequently, until the zucchini start to soften. Decrease the heat to medium-low, cover, and continue to cook for 5 minutes. Stir in the peas and warm through for 1 minute. Remove from the heat, stir in the basil, tarragon, and lemon zest, and set aside while you make the porridge.

2. To make the porridge, put the milk and water into a medium saucepan along with ¾ tsp salt and plenty of pepper. Bring to a boil over medium-high heat and add the semolina. Whisk continuously for 3–4 minutes, until smooth and thick, like porridge. Remove from the heat and stir in 3 oz/80g of the pecorino.

3. Divide the porridge among four (or six) shallow bowls and top with the zucchini and peas. Finish with the pine nuts, a sprinkle of the remaining pecorino, and drizzle with the oil.

Serves four to six

¼ **cup/50g unsalted butter**

5 garlic cloves, thinly sliced (3 tbsp)

6 large zucchini, trimmed, halved lengthwise, then thinly sliced widthwise (9 cups/1.2kg)

salt and black pepper

1⅔ **cups/200g frozen peas,** defrosted

1¼ **cups/25g basil leaves,** roughly shredded

¾ **cup/15g tarragon leaves**

1 lemon, finely zested to get 1 tsp

⅓ **cup plus 1 tbsp/ 50g pine nuts,** lightly toasted

1 tbsp olive oil

SEMOLINA PORRIDGE

2½ **cups/600ml whole milk**

2½ **cups/600 ml water**

1 cup plus 2 tbsp/ 180g semolina

3½ **oz/100g pecorino,** finely shaved

Roasted eggplant with anchovies and oregano

Serves four as a side

4 medium eggplants, sliced into ¾-inch/2cm rounds (2 lb 2 oz/1kg)

salt

7 tbsp/100ml olive oil

6 anchovy fillets in oil, drained and finely chopped (about 1 tbsp)

1 tbsp white wine vinegar

1 small garlic clove, minced

black pepper

1 tbsp oregano leaves

¼ cup/5g parsley leaves, roughly chopped

Anchovies and eggplant might sound like an unlikely combination, but it's one that really works. The anchovies bring more of a salty depth to the dish (rather than anything really fishy). This is lovely as it is, spooned on top of toasted sourdough, but also works as a side to all sorts of things. Roast chicken leftovers or a fresh tuna steak, for example. It keeps well in the fridge for up to 2 days; just bring back to room temperature before serving.

1. Preheat the oven to 450°F.

2. Mix the eggplant in a large bowl with ½ tsp of salt. Transfer to 2 large parchment-lined baking sheets and then brush with 5 tbsp/70ml of oil—you want it on both sides of the discs. Bake for 35 minutes, until dark golden brown and cooked through. Remove from the oven and set aside to cool.

3. In a small bowl, whisk together the anchovies, vinegar, garlic, ⅛ tsp of salt, and ¼ tsp of pepper. Slowly pour in the remaining 2 tbsp of oil, whisking continuously, until combined.

4. When ready to serve, finely chop the oregano and place in a large bowl along with the eggplant and parsley. Pour in the anchovy dressing, gently mix, and transfer to a platter or bowl.

Roasted eggplant with curried yogurt

All the various components of this dish can be prepared 1 day in advance, if you want to get ahead. Keep all the elements separate and in the fridge, bringing everything back to room temperature before you assemble the dish. When you next see some fresh curry leaves, grab hold of them—they are sometimes around, but then they disappear from the shelves for a while. Freeze what you don't use so that they're ready for when you next need them. Lightly fried in 1 tablespoon of oil, they make a wonderfully aromatic addition to this dish, sprinkled on top with the pomegranate seeds before serving. If you're going down the curry theme for the rest of your meal and have some papadums fried, these are great crumbled on top. If you do this, you won't need the almonds.

Serves four generously

3 large eggplants
  or 4 medium,
  (2 lb 6 oz/1.1kg)
7 tbsp/100ml peanut oil
salt and black pepper
⅔ cup/200g Greek-style yogurt
2 tsp medium curry powder
¼ tsp ground turmeric
1 large lime: zest to get 1 tsp, then juice to get 2 tsp

1 onion, thinly sliced (1⅔ cups/150g)
¼ cup/30g sliced almonds
½ tsp cumin seeds, toasted and lightly crushed
½ tsp coriander seeds, toasted and lightly crushed
¼ cup/40g pomegranate seeds

1. Preheat the oven to 450°F.

2. Use a vegetable peeler to peel away strips of eggplant skin from top to bottom, leaving the eggplants with alternating strips of black skin and white flesh, like a zebra. Cut widthwise into rounds, ¾ inch/2cm thick, and place in a large bowl. Mix well with 5 tbsp/70ml of the oil, ½ tsp of salt, and plenty of pepper, and spread out on a large parchment-lined baking sheet. Roast for 40–45 minutes, until dark golden brown, then set aside to cool.

3. Mix the yogurt with 1 tsp of curry powder, the turmeric, lime juice, a generous pinch of salt, and a good grind of pepper. Keep in the fridge, until required.

4. Put the remaining 2 tbsp of oil into a large frying pan and place over medium-high heat. Once hot, add the onion and fry for 8 minutes, stirring frequently, until soft and dark golden brown. Add the remaining 1 tsp of curry powder, the almonds, and a pinch of salt, and continue to fry for 2 minutes, until the almonds have lightly browned.

5. When you are ready to serve, arrange the eggplant slices on a large platter or individual plates, slightly overlapping. Spoon on the yogurt sauce and top with the fried onion mix. Sprinkle with the cumin seeds, coriander seeds, pomegranate seeds, and lime zest, and serve.

Grilled beefsteak tomatoes with chile, garlic, and ginger

Serves four

5 tbsp/75ml olive oil

3–4 mild red chiles,
sliced into ¼-inch/
½cm rounds, seeded
(mounded ½ cup/50g)

**1½-inch/4cm piece of
ginger,** finely cut into
thin strips (¼ cup/30g)

6-8 garlic cloves, thinly
sliced (3 tbsp)

**1 cup/20g cilantro
stems** (cut 1½ inches/
4cm long), plus ¼ **cup/
5g cilantro leaves** to
garnish

**2 lb 2 oz lbs/1kg
beefsteak tomatoes**
(4 tomatoes), sliced
crosswise into ½-inch/
1cm-thick rounds

**flaked sea salt and
black pepper**

**1½ tsp black mustard
seeds,** lightly toasted

These are delicious as they are, eaten with some bread alongside to mop up the oil. They can also be bulked into a punchy starter, with some burrata or mozzarella, or served for brunch with scrambled eggs. If your tomatoes are not perfectly ripe, just sprinkle them with a tiny pinch of sugar before broiling. These can be made up to 6 hours in advance and served at room temperature.

1. Preheat the broiler to high.

2. Pour the oil into a saucepan and place over medium-high heat. Add the chiles, ginger, and garlic and fry gently for 5 minutes, stirring every once in a while until the garlic is just starting to brown. Add the cilantro stalks and continue to fry for 2–3 more minutes, until the garlic is light golden brown and the chile is aromatic. Using a slotted spoon (so that you can preserve the oil), transfer the aromatics to a plate to stop them cooking. Set aside.

3. Arrange the tomato slices on a 12 x 16 inch/30 x 40cm baking sheet, so they are not overlapping. Brush with 2 tbsp of the aromatic oil, then sprinkle with 1½ tsp of flaked salt and a generous grind of pepper. Place the sheet about 2 inches/5cm beneath the broiler and cook for 10–12 minutes, until the tomatoes have started to brown. Remove the tomatoes from the oven, pour the remaining aromatic oil on top, sprinkle with the aromatics, and set aside for 10 minutes.

4. Serve the tomatoes on the baking sheet or transfer them to a large platter, overlapping them slightly. Scatter with the cilantro leaves and mustard seeds and pour any oil and juices remaining in the pan on top.

Hot, charred cherry tomatoes with cold yogurt

Serves four as a starter
or part of a mezze plate

12¼ oz/350g cherry
   tomatoes

3 tbsp olive oil

¾ tsp cumin seeds

½ tsp light brown sugar

3 garlic cloves, thinly
   sliced

3 thyme sprigs

6 oregano sprigs:
   3 sprigs left whole
   and the rest stemmed,
   to serve

1 lemon: finely shave the
   skin of ½ to get 3 strips,
   then finely grate the
   other ½ to get 1 tsp zest

flaked sea salt and
   black pepper

1⅔ cups/350g extra-
   thick Greek-style
   yogurt, fridge-cold

1 tsp Urfa chile flakes
   (or ½ tsp other crushed
   red pepper flakes)

One of the beauties of this dish lies in the exciting contrast between the hot, juicy tomatoes and fridge-cold yogurt, so make sure the tomatoes are straight out of the oven and the yogurt is straight out of the fridge. The heat of the tomatoes will make the cold yogurt melt, invitingly, so plenty of crusty sourdough or focaccia to mop it all up is a must alongside.

1. Preheat the oven to 425°F.

2. Place the tomatoes in a mixing bowl with the olive oil, cumin, sugar, garlic, thyme, oregano sprigs, lemon strips, ½ tsp of flaked salt, and a good grind of pepper. Mix to combine, then transfer to a baking sheet just large enough—about 6 x 8 inches/15 x 20cm—to fit all the tomatoes together snugly. Place the sheet about 2 inches/5cm beneath the broiler and roast for 20 minutes, until the tomatoes are beginning to blister and the liquid is bubbling. Turn the oven to the broil setting and broil for 6–8 minutes, until the tomatoes start to blacken on top.

3. While the tomatoes are roasting, combine the yogurt with the grated lemon zest and ¼ tsp of flaked salt. Keep in the fridge until ready to serve.

4. Once the tomatoes are ready, spread the chilled yogurt on a platter (with a lip) or in a wide, shallow bowl, creating a dip in it with the back of a spoon. Spoon the hot tomatoes on top, along with their juices, lemon strips, garlic, and herbs, and finish with the oregano leaves and chile flakes. Serve at once.

Tomato, chard, and spinach with toasted almonds

This is perfect served in all sorts of ways: warm as it is, along with some steamed rice, or sprinkled with feta. It's also good as an accompaniment to chicken or fish, served warm or at room temperature.

Once cooked, this can be kept for up 1 day in the fridge, just bring back to room temperature or warm through before serving, adding the almonds at the last minute.

Serves six as a side

¼ **cup/60ml olive oil**

½ **cup/50g sliced almonds**

½ **tsp paprika**

1½ **tsp caraway seeds**

2 **garlic cloves,** thinly sliced

2 **(14.5 oz/400g) cans plum tomatoes**

1 lb 2oz/500g **Swiss chard,** stalks thinly sliced and leaves roughly chopped

salt

4½ **oz/130g spinach,** roughly shredded

2 **limes:** finely zest to get 1 tsp, then juice to get 2 tbsp

1¾ **cups/35g mint,** roughly chopped

1¾ **cups/35g dill,** roughly chopped

8 **green onions,** chopped into ½-inch/1cm pieces (1 cup/80g)

1. Place a large sauté pan with a lid, over medium heat with 2 tbsp of the oil, the almonds, and paprika. Fry for 2–3 minutes, until the almonds are golden brown, then transfer to a bowl, discarding the oil once cooled.

2. Return the pan to medium-high heat with the remaining 2 tbsp of oil. Once hot, add the caraway and garlic and fry for 1 minute, until they start to sizzle and brown. Add the tomatoes with their juice, chard, and ¾ tsp of salt and stir through, crushing the tomatoes as you go. Cover the pan and continue to cook for 20 minutes, stirring every once in a while, until the chard wilts and the tomatoes break down. Remove from the heat, stir in the spinach, lime zest, lime juice, the mint, dill, and green onions. Serve with the almonds sprinkled on top.

Fried broccoli and kale with garlic, cumin, and lime

You can blanch the broccoli and kale well ahead of time here—a good few hours. Once half-cooked, and then refreshed and dried, it's ready for the final fry before serving. Doing this little bit of prep turns the dish into one that can get to the table in just over 5 minutes.

1. Place a large saucepan filled with plenty of salted water over high heat. Once boiling, add the broccoli and blanch for 90 seconds. Use a slotted spoon to remove the broccoli, then refresh under plenty of cold water and dry well. Keep the water at a boil and add the kale. Blanch for 30 seconds, then drain and refresh. Squeeze out as much water from the kale as you can with a clean kitchen towel and set aside.

2. Put the oil into a large sauté pan and place over high heat. Add the garlic and cumin and fry for about 2 minutes, stirring a few times, until the garlic is a light golden brown. Use a slotted spoon to remove the garlic and set aside. Add the kale to the oil—take care, it might spatter at the beginning—and fry for 3–4 minutes, until the leaves are starting to crisp. Add the broccoli, 1 tsp chile flakes, and ¼ tsp of salt. Stir through for a minute, then transfer to a large plate or dish. Gently mix in the mint and drizzle with the lime juice. Serve with the remaining 1 tsp chile flakes and the crisp garlic sprinkled on top.

Serves six as a side

1 large head of broccoli, cut into 1¼–1½ inch/3–4cm florets (3 cups/300g)

12¼ oz/350g curly kale, tough stems discarded and leaves torn into pieces (3¾ cups/250g)

3 tbsp olive oil

3 garlic cloves, thinly sliced

½ tsp cumin seeds

2 tsp Urfa chile flakes (or 1 tsp other crushed red pepper flakes)

salt

½ cup/10g mint leaves, roughly shredded

1 tbsp lime juice

Broccolini with soy sauce, garlic, and peanuts

Serves four as a side

3 tbsp peanut oil

3 garlic cloves, thinly
sliced

**1¼-inch/3cm piece of
ginger,** peeled and
julienned (2½ tbsp)

1 orange, peel finely
shaved to get 3 strips

**3 tbsp salted roasted
peanuts,** roughly
chopped

**1 lb 3 oz/550g
broccolini,** trimmed
and cut in half crosswise
if the stems are thick

2 tbsp light soy sauce

1½ tsp honey

salt

_This is also lovely with (an equal quantity of) choy sum, if you
prefer, instead of the broccolini. If you use choy sum it'll only need
1½ minutes of steaming. This is good as a side to all sorts of things—
any roasted bird, for example—as it is with a bowl of steamed rice._

1. Heat the oil in a small saucepan over medium-high heat.
Add the garlic, ginger, orange strips, and peanuts and fry for
2–3 minutes, stirring frequently, until the garlic and nuts are
light golden brown. Transfer to a small bowl (along with all
of the oil) to stop them cooking and set aside.

2. Place a steamer insert in a stockpot and fill with just enough
water so it doesn't touch the steaming basket. Place over high
heat and, once boiling, add the broccolini. Cover and steam for
4–5 minutes, until cooked. Remove from the heat, transfer to
a serving plate, and set aside.

3. Return the saucepan you cooked the peanuts in to high heat—
don't worry about wiping it clean—and add the soy sauce, honey,
and ⅛ tsp of salt. Heat for about 1 minute; it should reduce to
about 1½ tbsp of sauce. Spoon 2 tbsp of the infused oil over the
broccolini, along with the peanuts and aromatics. Add the reduced
soy sauce mixture, give everything a gentle mix, and serve.

Roast cabbage with tarragon and pecorino

Serves four as a side

½ **cup/120ml olive oil**

2 **extra-large lemons:**
finely zest to get 2 tbsp,
then juice to get 2 tbsp

2 **garlic cloves,** minced

salt and black pepper

2 **Napa cabbages,** outer
leaves discarded, then
cut lengthwise into
eighths (12 cups/1kg)

½ **cup/10g tarragon
leaves,** roughly
chopped

1 **oz/30g pecorino,**
shaved

This is served at room temperature so that the pecorino keeps its texture and flavor. It's perfect alongside a roast chicken or vegetables, along with mashed potatoes.

1. Preheat the oven to 450°F.

2. In a small bowl, whisk together the oil, lemon zest, garlic, ¼ tsp of salt, and a good grind of pepper. Set aside 2 tbsp.

3. Put the cabbage into a large bowl and season with ⅛ tsp of salt. Pour the oil mixture over the cabbage (the reserved 2 tbsp will be used later) and toss well to coat. Arrange on two parchment-lined baking sheets and roast for 20–25 minutes (rotating the sheets halfway through so that each sheet gets time near the top), until the edges are crisp and golden brown. Transfer the cabbage to a large platter and set aside for 5–10 minutes or so to cool slightly.

4. Add the lemon juice to the reserved 2 tbsp oil mixture and drizzle evenly over the cabbage pieces. Scatter the tarragon and pecorino over the top, add a good grind of pepper, and serve.

Pictured on page 98

Mustard-marinated kale with asparagus

There's a little bit of massaging and marinating here, but you can do this up to 4 hours in advance of serving, if you like. Just don't mix everything together until the last minute. Frozen shelled edamame are, happily, widely available in supermarkets.

1. Preheat the oven to 350°F.

2. Mix the sunflower and pumpkin seeds with ½ tsp of maple syrup, ⅛ tsp of salt, and a good grind of pepper. Spread out on a small parchment-lined baking sheet and bake for 12 minutes, until the seeds are golden brown. Set aside for about 30 minutes; the seeds will stick together as they cool and crisp up, but can then be broken into 1-inch/2½cm pieces.

3. Put the kale into a large bowl with the remaining 1 tsp of maple syrup, 2 tbsp of the oil, the vinegar, mustard, and ¼ tsp of salt. Mix together well, using your hands to massage the kale for about 1 minute, until it softens and takes on the flavors of the marinade. Set aside for at least 30 minutes (or up to 4 hours, if you want to get ahead).

4. Put the remaining 1 tbsp of oil into a large frying pan and place over medium-high heat. Add the asparagus and ⅛ tsp of salt and fry for 6 minutes, turning over throughout so that all sides start to brown and soften. Set aside to cool, then slice on an angle into 1½-inch/4cm pieces.

5. When ready to serve, add the asparagus, edamame, tarragon, and dill to the kale and mix well. Spread out on a large platter, sprinkle with the seeds, and serve.

Serves four to six as a side

3 tbsp sunflower seeds

3 tbsp pumpkin seeds

1½ tsp maple syrup

salt and black pepper

9 oz/250g kale, stems discarded, leaves torn roughly into 1½–2-inch/4–5cm pieces (3 cups/200g)

3 tbsp olive oil

1½ tbsp white wine vinegar

2 tsp whole-grain mustard

1 lb 2 oz/500g asparagus, woody ends trimmed (10 oz/300g)

4¼ oz/120g frozen shelled edamame, defrosted

½ cup/10g tarragon leaves, roughly chopped

¼ cup/5g dill, roughly chopped

Roasted asparagus with almonds, capers, and dill

This is a dish that my husband, Karl, cooks at home a lot on the weekend. He tends to be a bit more liberal on the butter front with his asparagus—what are weekends for, after all! And he is Irish! I've kept quantities just a little bit in check here.

Serves four as a side

1 lb 5 oz/600g asparagus, woody ends trimmed (14 oz/400g)

3 tbsp olive oil

salt and black pepper

2 tbsp unsalted butter

¼ **cup/20g sliced almonds**

3 tbsp baby capers (or regular capers), dried with a paper towel

½ **cup/10g dill,** roughly chopped

1. Preheat the oven to 425°F.

2. Mix the asparagus with 1 tbsp of oil, a generous pinch of salt, and a good grind of pepper. Arrange on a large parchment-lined baking sheet, spaced well apart, and roast for 8–12 minutes (timing will vary depending on the thickness of the stalks), until the asparagus is soft and starting to brown in places. Transfer to a large serving plate and set aside.

3. Put the butter into a small saucepan and place over medium-high heat. Once melted, add the almonds and fry for 1–2 minutes, stirring frequently, until the almonds are golden brown. Pour the almonds and butter evenly over the asparagus.

4. Add the remaining 2 tbsp of oil to the saucepan and place over high heat. Once hot, add the capers and fry for 1–2 minutes, stirring continuously, until they have opened up and become crisp. Using a slotted spoon, remove the capers from the oil and sprinkle them over the asparagus, along with the dill. Discard the oil and serve warm.

Cavolo nero with chorizo and preserved lemon

This delivers in so many ways: all the goodness of hearty dark green cavolo nero (also known as lacinato kale), all the pops of surprise from the preserved lemon, and all the tastiness that chorizo will always bring. The result can be served either as a stand-alone tapas or as a side to all sorts of grilled or roasted meat.

1. Put the oil into a large sauté pan with a lid and place over medium-high heat. Once hot, add the chorizo and fry for 3–4 minutes, until golden brown. Add the garlic and cook for 1 minute longer, until starting to brown. Stir in the paprika, then, using a slotted spoon, lift the chorizo and garlic out of the oil and place in a small bowl.

2. Add the cavolo nero to the pan, in three or four additions, stirring it into the oil. Once all the leaves have been added, add the water, ¼ tsp of salt, and plenty of pepper. Cook for 3 minutes, covered, stirring once or twice to help the leaves wilt. Remove the lid and continue to fry for 5–6 minutes, stirring frequently, until the liquid has evaporated and the leaves are cooked but still retain a slight bite and are starting to brown.

3. Return the chorizo and garlic to the pan, along with the preserved lemon and lemon juice. Stir through, then remove from the heat and add the sour cream. Fold through, to combine, then divide among four bowls or place on one large platter.

Serves four as a side

1 tbsp olive oil

2 fresh chorizo cooking sausages, halved lengthwise and cut into ½-inch/1cm rounds (1¼ cups/150g)

3 garlic cloves, thinly sliced

½ tsp sweet smoked paprika

1 lb 5 oz/600g cavolo nero (lacinato kale), leaves pulled off stems, stems discarded, leaves roughly chopped into 1½-inch/4cm strips and rinsed (5⅓ cups/360g)

2 tbsp water

salt and black pepper

2 small preserved lemons, seeds discarded, skin and flesh roughly chopped (¼ cup/40g)

1 tbsp lemon juice

⅓ cup plus 2 tbsp/100g sour cream

Quick okra with sweet-and-sour dressing

Serves four as a side

1½ lb/700g okra, stems trimmed (be careful not to expose the seeds, as this will make the dish "slimy")

3 tbsp peanut oil (or other mild oil)

2 garlic cloves, minced

salt and black pepper

1 red chile, seeded and thinly sliced

2 tsp maple syrup

1 large lime: finely zest to get 1 tsp, then juice to get 1½ tbsp

½ tsp sesame oil

¾ cup/15g cilantro, roughly chopped

⅓ cup/40g salted roasted peanuts, roughly chopped, to serve

Anyone who loves okra will never stop trying to convert those who think they don't love okra to the vegetable. Anyone put off by its sliminess (which results from it being chopped up and cooked) really should be open-minded here. The okra remains whole and is barely cooked, so the result is the opposite of what you might imagine. This is a lovely side to all sorts of dishes—it's perfect alongside the Whole roasted sea bass with soy sauce and ginger (page 260)—or as it is, with a bowl of plain rice.

1. Preheat the oven to 425°F.

2. Place the okra in a large bowl with 2 tbsp of oil, the garlic, ¾ tsp of salt, and a good grind of black pepper. Spread out on two parchment-lined baking sheets—you don't want them to be overcrowded—and roast for 7 minutes, until just slightly cooked but still firm and bright green in color. Remove from the oven and set aside to cool for 10 minutes.

3. Place the remaining 1 tbsp of oil in a large bowl with the chile, maple syrup, lime zest, lime juice, sesame oil, and ⅛ tsp salt. Mix to combine, then, just before serving, add the okra and cilantro. Mix really well—the dressing tends to sink to the bottom of the bowl and you don't want to lose any of it—then transfer to a serving bowl.

4. Sprinkle the roasted peanuts over the top and serve.

Pictured on page 88

Garry's stir-fried cabbage with garlic and chile

This is, as my friend Garry Bar-Chang showed me when he was cooking up a Taiwanese feast, a very easy way to eat a lot of cabbage. The secret lies in there being lots of chile, lots of garlic, and lots of stir-frying.

1. Put the oil into a large sauté pan or wok and place over high heat. Once hot, add the garlic and chiles and fry for 1 minute, stirring continuously, until the garlic starts to turn golden. Add the green onions and cook for another 2 minutes, continuing to stir.

2. Add the cabbage in stages (it shrinks as it cooks down), along with ¾ tsp salt. Cook for about 5 minutes, stirring, until the cabbage is cooked and soft but still retains a bite. Remove from the heat and set aside for 5 minutes before serving, along with the wedges of lime.

Serves four as a side

2½ tbsp sunflower oil

6 garlic cloves, sliced (3 tbsp)

2 red chiles, seeded and cut into roughly ¾-inch/2cm pieces

5 green onions, cut on an angle into 1¼-inch/ 3cm pieces

1 Napa cabbage, leaves separated and roughly torn in half (1 lb 3 oz/550g)

salt

1 lime, quartered, to serve

Pictured on page 89

Cauliflower, pomegranate, and pistachio salad

It was a little moment of revelation, I remember, when I first combined roasted cauliflower and raw grated cauliflower in the same dish. So different from one another, but working so well combined. This is lovely as it is, served as part of a spread, or spooned alongside some roast chicken or lamb. Don't throw away the leaves of the cauliflower here. They're delicious to eat, roasted and crisp, or grated raw as you would the rest of the cauliflower. If you want to get ahead, roast the cauliflower up to 4–6 hours in advance. Keep at room temperature and then just combine with the remaining ingredients when ready to serve.

1. Preheat the oven to 425°F.

2. Coarsely grate a third of the cauliflower and set aside in a bowl. Break the remaining cauliflower into florets, roughly 1¼ inches/3cm wide, and add these to a separate bowl with the cauliflower leaves, if you have any, and the onion. Toss everything together with 2 tbsp of oil and ¼ tsp of salt, then spread out on a large parchment-lined baking sheet. Roast for about 20 minutes, until cooked through and golden brown. Remove from the oven and set aside to cool.

3. Once cool, put the roasted vegetables into a large bowl with the 3 tbsp/50ml oil, the grated cauliflower, and parsley, mint, tarragon, pomegranate seeds, pistachios, cumin, and lemon juice, along with ¼ tsp salt. Toss gently, just to combine, then transfer to a platter and serve.

Serves four

1 extra-large cauliflower (1¾ lb/800g)

1 small onion, roughly sliced (¾ cup/130g)

⅓ **cup/80ml olive oil**

salt

1¼ **cups/25g parsley,** roughly chopped

½ **cup/10g mint,** roughly chopped

½ **cup/10g tarragon,** roughly chopped

seeds from ½ medium pomegranate (mounded ½ cup/80g)

⅓ **cup/40g shelled pistachios,** lightly toasted and roughly chopped

1 tsp ground cumin

1½ **tbsp lemon juice**

Mustardy cauliflower cheese

Serves four

1 large cauliflower,
broken into roughly
1½ inch/4cm florets
(7 cups/700g)

2 tbsp/30g unsalted
butter

1 small onion, finely
diced (1 cup/120g)

1½ tsp cumin seeds

1 tsp medium curry
powder

1 tsp mustard powder

2 green chiles, seeded
and finely diced

¾ tsp black mustard
seeds

¾ cup plus 2 tbsp/
200ml heavy cream

4¼ oz/120g aged
Cheddar, coarsely
grated

salt

⅓ cup/15g fresh white
breadcrumbs (from
about ½ slice, crust left
on if soft)

¼ cup/5g parsley, finely
chopped

This is the ultimate comfort dish, looking for a roast chicken, some sausages, or a pan-fried steak to go alongside. Veggie options also work well—just some hearty brown rice, for example, and a simple salad with a dollop of yogurt and a wedge of lime. This can be made up to the point of baking and stored in the fridge for 1 day.

1. Preheat the oven to 400°F.

2. Steam the cauliflower over boiling water for 5 minutes, until just softening. Remove and set aside to cool slightly.

3. Put the butter into a 9-inch/24cm round casserole pan or oven-proof dish of a similar size and place over medium heat. Add the onion and sauté for 8 minutes, until soft and golden. Add the cumin, curry powder, mustard powder, and chiles and cook for 4 minutes, stirring occasionally. Add the mustard seeds, cook for 1 minute, then pour in the cream. Add 1¼ cups/100g of Cheddar and ½ tsp of salt and simmer for 2–3 minutes, until the sauce slightly thickens. Add the cauliflower, stir gently, and simmer for 1 minute before removing from the heat.

4. Place the remaining ¼ cup/20g of Cheddar in a bowl and add the breadcrumbs and parsley. Mix, then sprinkle over the cauliflower. Wipe the top inside edge of the pan clean (with a spatula or cloth)—any cream there will burn—and place in the oven. Bake for 8 minutes, until the sauce is bubbling and the cauliflower is hot. Turn the broiler to high and keep the pan underneath for 4 minutes, or until the top is golden and crisp. Keep an eye on it so that it does not burn. Remove from the oven and allow to cool a little—just for 5 minutes or so—before serving.

Roasted whole cauliflower

Serves four

1 jumbo cauliflower,
with all leaves intact
(2¾ lb/1.3kg)

3 tbsp unsalted butter,
at room temperature

2 tbsp olive oil

flaked sea salt

1 lemon, cut into
wedges, to serve

Green tahini sauce
(optional; recipe
follows)

Keep all the leaves on the head of cauliflower—they are deliciously crisp and tasty when roasted. I like to serve this in the center of the table, for people to share with drinks at the start of a meal. We break the cauliflower apart with our hands, dipping the individual florets and crispy green leaves into the green tahini sauce and sprinkling with salt. If that sounds a bit odd or messy (which it's actually not, surprisingly), you can always cut the cauliflower into four wedges and serve on individual plates, to be eaten more traditionally with a knife and fork! Either way, the tahini sauce is entirely optional. I love it, but just a squeeze of lemon or a dollop of crème fraîche also work very well.

1. Using a pair of scissors, lightly trim the leaves at the top of the cauliflower, so that about 2 inches/5cm of the actual cauliflower head is exposed.

2. Fill a pan (that is large enough to fit the cauliflower in) three-quarters full of salted water. Bring to a boil, then carefully lower in the cauliflower, exposed head down—don't worry if the base is sticking out a little. Return to a boil, cook for 6 minutes, then use a slotted spoon to transfer the cauliflower into a colander, exposed head down. Set aside for 10 minutes to drain and cool.

3. Preheat the oven to 375°F.

4. Mix together the butter and oil. Place the cauliflower on a medium baking sheet, exposed head now facing upwards, and spread the butter-oil mix all over the cauliflower, followed by 1¼ tsp of flaked salt. Place in the oven and roast for 1½–2 hours,

Pictured on pages 96–97

basting the cauliflower with the oil five or six times during cooking, until the cauliflower is really tender and dark golden brown and the leaves are crisp and charred.

5. Remove from the oven and set aside for 5 minutes, then cut into wedges (or pull it apart with your hands!). Serve with the lemon wedges and a little sprinkle of salt, or the green tahini sauce below.

Green tahini sauce

This is a delicious sauce to serve with the cauliflower, but is totally optional. It will keep in the fridge for up to 3 days.

1. Pour the tahini into the small bowl of a food processor along with the parsley and garlic. Blitz for about 1 minute, until the tahini is green, then pour in the water and lemon juice and season with ¼ tsp of flaked salt. Continue to blitz until you have a smooth green sauce with the consistency of heavy cream. Add a touch more tahini if it's too thin, or a splash more water if it's too thick.

This makes enough sauce for one cauliflower, to serve four

rounded ¼ cup/ 80g tahini

¾ cup/15g parsley, roughly chopped

1 small garlic clove, crushed

⅓ cup/80ml water

3 tbsp lemon juice

flaked sea salt

Curried egg and cauliflower salad

This is what Coronation chicken would taste like if you replaced the chicken with cauliflower and hard-boiled egg. An introduction that possibly makes no sense until you eat it for yourself. If you are missing the chicken side of the equation, then you could do worse than serve this with said bird, roasted on the weekend.

Serves four to six

1 medium cauliflower, trimmed and broken into 1¼–1½-inch/3–4cm florets (5 cups/500g); keeping the tender leaves

1 onion, peeled and cut into ½-inch/1cm wedges (2 cups/180g)

2 tbsp olive oil

1 tbsp mild curry powder

salt and black pepper

9 large eggs

6 tbsp/100g Greek-style yogurt

3 tbsp mayonnaise

1 tsp Aleppo chile flakes (or ½ tsp other crushed red pepper flakes)

1 tsp cumin seeds, toasted and roughly crushed

2 lemons: 1 squeezed to get 1 tbsp juice, 1 cut into 4–6 wedges, to serve

½ cup/10g tarragon, roughly chopped

1. Preheat the oven to 475°F.

2. Mix the cauliflower florets (with any young leaves attached) in a large bowl with the onion, oil, 2 tsp of the curry powder, ¾ tsp of salt, and plenty of pepper. Once combined, spread out on a large parchment-lined baking sheet and roast for 15 minutes, until soft and golden brown but still retaining a bite. Remove from the oven and set aside to cool.

3. Fill a medium pan with plenty of water and bring to a boil over high heat. Decrease the heat to medium-high, then carefully lower in the eggs and boil gently for 10 minutes, until hard-boiled. Drain the eggs, then return them to the same pan and fill with cold water to stop them cooking. Once cool, peel the eggs, place them in a large bowl, and break them roughly with the back of a fork to form large chunks.

4. In a separate small bowl, mix together the yogurt, mayonnaise, the remaining 1 tsp of curry powder, half the chile flakes, the cumin, lemon juice, and ¼ tsp salt. Add the sauce to the eggs, along with the cauliflower and onion and the tarragon. Mix together well, spoon the mixture onto a large plate, then sprinkle with the remaining chile flakes and serve, along with the lemon wedges.

Chickpeas and Swiss chard with yogurt

Serves two

2 carrots, peeled and chopped into ¾-inch/2cm pieces (1½ cups/200g)

3 tbsp olive oil, plus extra to serve

salt and black pepper

1 large onion, finely chopped (1¼ cups/180g)

1 tsp caraway seeds

1½ tsp ground cumin

7 oz/200g Swiss chard leaves, sliced into ½-inch/1cm strips

1 (15.5 oz/440g) can chickpeas, drained and rinsed (1¾ cups/240g)

5 tbsp/75 ml water

1 lemon: juice half to get 1 tbsp and cut the other half into 2 wedges, to serve

¼ cup/70g Greek-style yogurt

¼ cup/5g cilantro, roughly chopped

This is comfort food at its best, served with some steamed rice. Don't worry if you don't have cilantro at home already—it's a nice little garnish but the dish holds its own perfectly without. Make this up to 6 hours ahead if you like, up to the point before the lemon juice and yogurt are added. Assemble before serving and serve at room temperature or just warmed through.

1. Preheat the oven to 425°F.

2. Mix the carrots with 1 tbsp of oil, ¼ tsp of salt, and a grind of pepper. Spread out on a parchment-lined baking sheet and roast for 20 minutes—they should still be a little crunchy.

3. Place the remaining 2 tbsp of oil in a large frying pan, over medium heat, and add the onion, caraway, and cumin. Fry for 10 minutes, stirring occasionally, until golden brown. Add the chard, cooked carrots, chickpeas, water, ½ tsp salt, and a good grind of pepper and mix through. Cook for 5 minutes, until the chard leaves are soft and hardly any juice is left in the pan.

4. Remove from the heat, stir in the lemon juice, top with a generous spoonful of yogurt, a sprinkle of cilantro, a drizzle of oil, and a wedge of lemon and serve.

Pictured on page 102

Slow-cooked runner beans in tomato sauce

Serve this with some brown rice for a dish that manages to be both summery and light, comforting and hearty. It's lovely, also, as part of a mezze spread. It can be made up to 2 days in advance, if you like— the flavors only improve. You can then either warm it through before serving or take it out of the fridge 30 minutes or so before eating to have it come to room temperature.

1. Put the oil into a large sauté pan with a lid and place over medium-high heat. Add the onions and fry gently for 8 minutes, stirring from time to time, until they are starting to color and soften. Add the garlic, cumin, paprika, and nutmeg and continue to cook for another 2 minutes, stirring. Add the tomato paste and cook for another 1 minute, then add the beans, tomatoes, stock, ¾ tsp of salt, and some black pepper. Decrease the heat to medium, cover the pan, and simmer, covered, for 30 minutes.

2. Remove the lid and simmer for another 30 minutes, stirring from time to time, until the sauce is thick and the beans are completely soft. Remove from the heat and stir in the cilantro. Serve warm or at room temperature.

Serves four

2 tbsp olive oil

2 onions, roughly chopped (1¾ cups/240g)

3 large garlic cloves, minced

2 tsp cumin seeds

1½ tsp hot paprika

¾ tsp ground nutmeg

1 tbsp tomato paste

1 lb 2 oz/500g runner beans, trimmed and sliced on the diagonal into ¾-inch/2cm pieces

6 medium tomatoes, peeled and roughly chopped (2½ cups/500g)

2 cups/500ml vegetable stock

salt and black pepper

½ cup/10g cilantro, roughly chopped

Tofu and haricots verts with chraimeh sauce

Serves four

**1 lb/455g haricots
  verts,** trimmed

1 tbsp sunflower oil

14 oz/400g firm tofu,
  cut into 1-inch/2½cm
  cubes and patted dry

salt

¾ cup/15g cilantro,
  roughly chopped

CHRAIMEH SAUCE

6 garlic cloves, minced

2 tsp hot paprika

1 tbsp caraway seeds,
  lightly toasted and
  crushed in a pestle
  and mortar

2 tsp ground cumin

½ tsp ground cinnamon

3 tbsp sunflower oil

3 tbsp tomato paste

2 tsp sugar

2 limes: juice 1 to get
  1 tbsp and cut the other
  into 4 wedges, to serve

salt

**1 cup plus 1 tbsp/
  250ml water**

*This is a lovely veggie main, served as it is or with some rice.
Chraimeh is a piquant sauce from Libya. It keeps well in the fridge
for at least 1 week (or can also be frozen and kept for 1 month),
so make double or triple the quantities. It also works as a sauce
for chicken or fish or just as a dip with bread before supper.*

1. Fill a medium saucepan halfway with water and place over
high heat. Once boiling, add the green beans and boil for
5–6 minutes, until they are cooked but still retain a slight bite.
Drain, refresh with cold water, drain again, and set aside.

2. Put the oil into a large sauté pan and place over medium-high
heat. Once hot, add the tofu and a rounded ¼ tsp of salt and fry
for 4–5 minutes, turning throughout so that all sides are golden
brown. Remove from the pan and set aside.

3. To make the chraimeh sauce, mix the garlic, paprika, caraway,
cumin, cinnamon, and oil in a small bowl. Return the large sauté
pan to medium-high heat and, once hot, add the garlic and spice
mix. Fry for about 1 minute, then add the tomato paste, sugar, lime
juice, and ¾ tsp of salt. Stir to combine, then pour in the water
to make a thin sauce. Once bubbling, stir frequently for about
2 minutes, until the sauce begins to thicken. Return the green beans
to the pan and continue to cook for another 1 minute, until the
sauce is thick and the beans are hot.

4. Remove from the heat and gently stir in the tofu and cilantro.
Divide among four shallow bowls and serve, with a wedge of
lime alongside.

Avocado and fava bean mash

Serves four as part of a mezze plate

9 oz/250g podded fava beans, still in their shells but not in their pods (fresh or frozen)

1 large avocado, peeled and roughly chopped (1¼ cups/190g)

1 lemon: finely shave to get 1 long strip, then juice to get 1½ tbsp

¼ **cup/60ml olive oil**

salt

2 green onions, thinly sliced

You can look at shelling fava beans two ways: either as a great big bother not worth doing, or as something wonderfully therapeutic to do with the radio or music on. It's also a job very easy to outsource, if anyone is offering to help. Either way, the resulting dish is wonderful—lighter than an avocado-only guacamole and all the more lovely for it. The mash can be made in advance, if you like; it keeps in the fridge for a couple of days.

1. Fill a small saucepan with salted water and bring to a boil. Blanch the beans for 2 minutes, then drain, refresh, and drain again. Peel off and discard the skins of the beans, then set aside ⅓ cup/50g. Put the rest of the beans into a food processor with the avocado, lemon juice, 2 tbsp of oil, and ¼ tsp salt and blitz until almost smooth.

2. Heat the remaining 2 tbsp of oil in a small frying pan over medium-high heat, then gently fry the green onions and lemon strip for 1 minute. Remove from the heat and stir in the reserved fava beans and a pinch of salt.

3. Spread the avocado and fava bean mash over a plate creating a natural rim around the edge. Spoon the green onion mix into the middle just before serving. The lemon strip does not normally get eaten, but it looks nice as a garnish.

Pictured on page 108

Lima bean mash with muhammara

Muhammara is a spicy Levantine dip made from red peppers and walnuts. It keeps in the fridge for 3 days, so double the recipe, if you like—it's as lovely spread on a cheese sandwich or served with grilled meat as it is as a dip. I've left the skins on the peppers for ease, but remove them if you don't want the texture. The mash can be made 3 days in advance; keep in the fridge in a separate container and bring back to room temperature before serving.

1. Preheat the oven to 450°F.

2. Mix the peppers and oil and spread out on a large parchment-lined baking sheet. Roast for 15 minutes, and then add the garlic. Continue to roast for 15 minutes, until the skin of the peppers is soft and starting to blacken and the garlic is golden brown.

3. Place the peppers in a food processor, along with the garlic, thyme, paprika, pepper flakes, vinegar, all but 2 tbsp of the walnuts, and ½ tsp of salt. Blitz to form a rough paste and set aside.

4. To make the mash, put the oil into a small saucepan and place over medium heat. Once hot, add the garlic and thyme sprigs and fry very gently for 2–3 minutes, until the garlic starts to caramelize. Discard the garlic and set the sprigs of thyme aside, along with 2 tsp of the oil. Pour the remaining oil into a food processor with the lima beans, water, and ½ tsp of salt. Blitz until completely smooth, adding a little more water if you need to. Spread out on a large platter or a few plates, creating a natural rim around the edge, and spoon the muhammara into the center. Top with the crispy thyme springs, their reserved oil, and the remaining 2 tbsp of the walnuts and serve.

Serves six to eight

MUHAMMARA

5 red bell peppers, quartered, seeds and 1 stem discarded (10 cups/850g)

1 tbsp olive oil, plus extra to serve

8 garlic cloves, peeled

1 tbsp thyme leaves

¾ tsp sweet smoked paprika

¼ tsp crushed red pepper flakes

2 tsp balsamic vinegar

⅔ cup/60g walnut halves, lightly roasted and roughly chopped

salt

MASH

7 tbsp/100ml olive oil

1 garlic clove, skin on and lightly crushed

3 thyme sprigs

2 (15.5 oz/440g) cans lima beans, drained and rinsed (2¾ cups/ 470g drained weight)

1 tbsp water

salt

Pictured on page 109

Two bean and two lime salad

Making this ahead of time is fine—just hold back on the lime juice until before you serve. It will keep for up to 6 hours in the fridge. If you can't get hold of fresh or frozen kaffir lime leaves, don't use freeze-dried—the leaves are too brittle to work when finely chopped. As an alternative, use either a stick of lemongrass (remove the tough outer skin and finely chop the soft inner flesh) or else just stick with the lime zest and juice already listed—the dish will still pack a punch.

1. Roll up all the kaffir leaves into a thick cigar shape. Slice as thinly as possible, then finely chop the strips. Place in the bowl of a food processor with the lime zest, 1 cup/20g of cilantro, the mint, garlic, olive oil, chile, and ½ tsp of salt. Blitz until smooth, then set aside.

2. Bring a large pan of salted water to a boil and add the green beans. Blanch for 3 minutes, then add the edamame and cook for 1 minute. Drain all together, refresh under cold water, and set aside to dry.

3. Spoon the lime paste over the beans, add the lime juice, and stir to combine. Sprinkle with the sesame seeds, along with the remaining ½ cup/5g of cilantro, and serve at once.

Serves four as a starter or side

6 large kaffir lime leaves (fresh or frozen), stems removed

2 large limes: finely zest to get 1½ tsp, then juice to get 2 tbsp

1½ cups/30g cilantro, roughly chopped

½ cup/10g mint leaves

1 garlic clove, crushed

¼ cup/60ml olive oil

2 green chiles, seeded and thinly sliced

salt

1 lb 5oz/600g haricots verts, trimmed

5¼ oz/150g frozen shelled edamame (or peas)

1 tsp black sesame seeds

Mushrooms and chestnuts with za'atar

Serves six as a side

1 lb 6 oz/650g portobello mushrooms (about 6–8), cut into 1¼-inch/3cm wedges

7 oz/200g small shallots, peeled and left whole

5¼ oz/150g ready-cooked and peeled chestnuts, broken in half

¼ cup/5g sage leaves, roughly chopped

¼ cup/60ml olive oil, plus 2 tsp, to serve

2 garlic cloves, minced

salt and black pepper

¼ cup/5g tarragon leaves, roughly chopped

1 tbsp za'atar

2 tsp lemon juice

These are lovely as an autumn or festive side. They are also great for breakfast, served with scrambled eggs. Use any mushrooms—or a mix of mushrooms—depending on what you see. Just keep the net weight the same. If you've got large shallots lying around, they are fine to use—just cut them in half or even into quarters.

If you want to get ahead, prepare this up to 4 hours in advance—just place everything on the baking sheet, minus the salt and pepper, ready to be seasoned before roasting.

1. Preheat the oven to 450°F.

2. In a large bowl, mix the mushrooms, shallots, chestnuts, sage, oil, and garlic with ¾ tsp salt and lots of pepper. Spread on a large parchment-lined baking sheet and roast for 25 minutes, until the mushrooms and shallots are caramelized and soft. Remove from the oven and set aside to cool for 5 minutes.

3. Tip the warm mushrooms and chestnuts into a large bowl and mix in the tarragon, za'atar, lemon juice, and the 2 tsp of oil. Spoon into a large shallow bowl and serve.

Pictured on page 114

Brussels sprouts with browned butter and black garlic

Black garlic has a highly concentrated taste—licorice meets balsamic meets the absolute essence of garlic. It's a quick way to inject a huge amount of flavor into a dish. Get everything chopped and ready for this dish before you start, but don't cook it until just before serving— you want the sprouts to be eaten fresh from the pan.

1. Preheat the oven to 450°F.

2. Mix the sprouts with the oil and ¼ tsp of salt, then spread out on a parchment-lined baking sheet. Roast for 10 minutes, until the sprouts are golden brown but still crunchy.

3. Meanwhile, lightly crush the caraway seeds with a pestle and mortar. Add the black garlic and thyme and crush them to form a rough paste.

4. Put the butter into a large sauté pan and place over medium-high heat. Cook for 3 minutes, until melted and dark brown. Add the crushed garlic paste, sprouts, pumpkin seeds, and ⅛ tsp salt. Stir for 30 seconds, then remove from the heat. Stir in the lemon juice and transfer to a large bowl or individual plates. Drizzle with the tahini and serve at once.

Serves four as a side

1 lb/455g Brussels sprouts, trimmed and cut in half lengthwise (4 cups/400g)

1 tbsp olive oil

salt

¾ tsp caraway seeds

¾ oz/20g black garlic cloves (about 12), roughly chopped

2 tbsp thyme leaves

2 tbsp/30g unsalted butter

3 tbsp/30g pumpkin seeds, toasted

1½ tsp lemon juice

1 tbsp tahini

Pictured on page 115

Roasted baby carrots with harissa and pomegranate

Serves four as a side

2 tsp cumin seeds

2 tsp honey

2 tbsp rose harissa
(or 50 percent more
or less, depending on
variety; see page 301)

1½ tbsp unsalted butter,
melted

1 tbsp olive oil

salt

**1¾ lb/800g long, thin
baby carrots** (or
regular carrots, cut into
long batons, 4 x ½ inch/
10 x 1½cm), peeled
and stems trimmed
(to leave just a little bit)

**½ cup/10g cilantro
leaves,** roughly chopped

**½ cup/60g pomegranate
seeds** (from
½ pomegranate)

2 tsp lemon juice

This is a striking salad with bright colors and serious flavor. Serve alongside any chicken, slow-cooked lamb, or with a selection of vegetables and legumes. Long baby carrots look lovely here, as ever, but if you are starting with regular carrots that's fine— just slice them into long, thin batons.

Roast the carrots up to 6 hours in advance if you want to get ahead, and mix with the remaining ingredients just before you are ready to serve.

1. Preheat the oven to 475°F.

2. In a large bowl, mix the cumin, honey, harissa, butter, oil, and ¾ tsp salt. Add the carrots, mix well, then spread out on a large parchment-lined baking sheet. You don't want to overcrowd the carrots, so use two sheets if you need to.

3. Roast for 12–14 minutes, until the carrots are beginning to brown but still retain a bite, then remove from the oven and set aside to cool.

4. When ready to serve, mix the carrots with the cilantro, pomegranate seeds, and lemon juice and serve.

Carrot salad with yogurt and cinnamon

Serves four as a side

2 lb 2 oz/1kg long, thin baby carrots, unpeeled but scrubbed, stalk trimmed to about 1¼ inches/3cm

3 tbsp olive oil

1½ tbsp apple cider vinegar

1 tsp honey

1 garlic clove, minced

⅛ tsp ground cinnamon

salt and black pepper

½ cup/120g Greek-style yogurt

¼ cup/60g crème fraîche

¼ cup/5g dill, roughly chopped

½ cup/10g cilantro, roughly chopped

I love the look of the long, thin baby carrots here, but don't worry if you don't have any. Regular carrots, halved or quartered lengthwise, work just fine. This is a lovely colorful addition to all sorts of feasts: great served alongside the couscous and tomato salad (page 158), as just one example, and the slow-cooked lamb (page 215). Steam the carrots and make the dressing 6 hours in advance, or even up to 1 day ahead if keeping in the fridge. Bring back to room temperature, adding the yogurt and herbs when ready to serve.

1. Place the carrots in a steamer and steam for 8–12 minutes (depending on thickness), until they are cooked through but still retain a bite.

2. Meanwhile, whisk together the olive oil, vinegar, honey, garlic, cinnamon, ½ tsp salt, and lots of pepper in a large bowl. Once combined, add the carrots as soon as they are cooked. Mix well and set aside to cool.

3. Mix together the yogurt and crème fraîche in a medium bowl with ¼ tsp of salt. Add this to the carrots, along with the dill and cilantro. Stir through gently—you don't want to overmix. Transfer carefully to a serving bowl and serve.

Pictured on page 120

Roasted butternut squash with lentils and dolcelatte

I like to serve this with the squash and lentils still a little warm—so that the cheese slightly melts when it's dotted on top—but it also works at room temperature, if you want to make it in advance. Make up to the point of adding the dolcelatte and set aside for up to 6 hours. Add the final elements just before serving.

If you start with ready-cooked lentils, then skip the stage where they get simmered and just add them straight to the bowl with the lemon, garlic, herbs, and so forth.

1. Preheat the oven to 450°F.

2. Place the squash and onions in a large bowl with 2 tbsp of oil, the sage leaves, ¾ tsp of salt, and plenty of pepper. Mix well, then spread out on a large parchment-lined baking sheet. Roast for 25–30 minutes, until cooked and golden brown. Remove from the oven and set aside to cool for 10 minutes.

3. While the squash is in the oven, fill a medium saucepan halfway with water (if starting with dried lentils rather than ready-cooked) and place over high heat. Once boiling, add the lentils, decrease the heat to medium, and simmer for 20 minutes, until cooked. Drain, set aside to cool slightly, then place in a large bowl. Stir in the lemon zest, lemon juice, garlic, parsley, mint, tarragon, remaining 1 tbsp of oil, and ¼ tsp of salt.

4. Add the squash and onion to the lentils and stir gently. Transfer to a serving bowl, dot with dolcelatte, drizzle with oil, and serve.

Serves six as a side

1 large butternut squash, unpeeled, halved lengthwise, seeded and cut into ½-inch/1cm-thick half-moons or wedges (2 lb 1½ oz/950g)

2 red onions, cut into 1¼-inch/3cm-wide wedges (3½ cups/320g)

3 tbsp olive oil, plus extra to serve

½ cup/10g sage leaves

salt and black pepper

½ cup/100g Puy lentils (or 3 cups/235g if starting with ready-cooked)

1 large lemon: finely zest to get 2 tsp, then juice to get 2 tbsp

1 garlic clove, minced

¼ cup/5g parsley leaves, roughly chopped

¼ cup/5g mint leaves, roughly chopped

½ cup/10g tarragon leaves, roughly chopped

3½ oz/100g dolcelatte or gorgonzola cheese, torn into ¾ inch/2cm pieces (optional)

Pictured on page 121

Butternut squash with corn salsa, feta, and pumpkin seeds

Serves six as a side

1 extra-large butternut squash, unpeeled, halved lengthwise, seeded and cut into wedges, about 3¼ inches/8cm long and 1¼ inches/3cm wide (2¾ lb/1.3kg)

5 tbsp/75ml olive oil, plus extra to serve

salt and black pepper

2 ears corn, husks removed and any silk discarded

1 large red chile, seeded and finely diced

3 limes: finely zest 1 to get 2 tsp, then juice to get ¼ cup

½ cup/10g cilantro, roughly chopped

¼ cup/5g mint leaves, roughly shredded

3 tbsp pumpkin seeds, toasted

1¾ oz/50g feta, roughly crumbled into ½–¾-inch/1–2cm pieces

You'll get more of a bite on your charred corn if you start with fresh kernels, as I do here, but you can also use 2⅓ cups/300g of frozen kernels, defrosted, as an alternative, and fry them in a pan. The result is more chewy, but it still works. Make all the various elements up to 1 day in advance, if you like—the squash, the salsa, the feta, and the seeds—and just bring everything back to room temperature and assemble the dish before serving. You don't need to serve it straightaway, though; it can sit around for a good couple of hours if need be.

1. Preheat the oven to 450°F.

2. Mix the butternut squash with 2 tbsp of oil, ½ tsp of salt, and plenty of pepper. Spread out on a large parchment-lined baking sheet, skin side down and spaced well apart. Roast for 25 minutes, until the squash is cooked through and golden brown. Remove from the oven and set aside to cool.

3. Place a grill pan over high heat and ventilate your kitchen well. Add the corn and grill for about 8 minutes, turning over throughout so that they are charred all over. Remove from the heat and, once cool enough to handle, place the corn perpendicular to a chopping board and use a sharp knife to shave the corn kernels off the cob. Place the kernels in a bowl with the chile, lime zest, lime juice, the remaining 3 tbsp of oil, ¼ tsp of salt, and the cilantro and mint. Mix well and set aside.

4. Arrange the squash on separate plates or on one large platter. Spoon the salsa on top, sprinkle the pumpkin seeds, dot with the feta, and serve, drizzled with a little extra oil.

Roasted beets with yogurt and preserved lemon

This is a match made in heaven served alongside some oily fish—a smoked mackerel or trout fillet, for example—or some steamed salmon. It's also great served over freshly cooked lentils. You can make the salad in advance—the day before serving, even. If you do so, just hold back on the dill and the tahini yogurt and keep everything in the fridge until ready to serve.

1. Preheat the oven to 450°F.

2. Wrap the beets individually in foil, place on a baking sheet and roast for 30–60 minutes, depending on size, until a knife inserted goes through smoothly. When cool enough to handle, peel off the skin and cut each beet into ¼-inch/½cm slices. Place in a large mixing bowl and set aside to cool.

3. Put the olive oil into a small frying pan and place over medium heat. Add the cumin seeds and cook for about 3 minutes, until they start to pop. Pour the seeds and oil over the beets along with the onion, preserved lemon, lemon juice, ½ cup/10g of the dill, 1 tsp of salt, and a grind of black pepper. Mix everything together well, then transfer the salad to a large serving plate.

4. Stir the tahini into the yogurt and dot this over the beets in four or five places. Stir minimally—you want the yogurt and beets to mix only slightly—then sprinkle with the remaining ¼ cup/5g of dill.

Serves four as a side

2lb 2 oz/1kg beets, unpeeled but scrubbed

2 tbsp olive oil

1½ tsp cumin seeds

1 small red onion, very thinly sliced (mounded 1 cup/100g)

1 small preserved lemon, skin and flesh finely chopped and seeds discarded (¼ cup/40g)

2 tbsp lemon juice

¾ cup/15g dill, roughly shredded

salt and black pepper

1 tbsp tahini

½ cup/150g Greek-style yogurt

Whole-roasted celery root with coriander seed oil

Serves four as a starter or side

I large celery root, hairy roots discarded (no need to trim) unpeeled but scrubbed clean (2½ lb/1.2kg)

3 tbsp olive oil, plus extra to serve

I½ tsp coriander seeds, lightly crushed

flaked sea salt

I lemon, cut into wedges, to serve

I've managed to achieve the seemingly impossible here, of taking a recipe from my NOPI cookbook (full of recipes that would not make it into Ottolenghi SIMPLE) and actually making it more complicated for Ottolenghi SIMPLE. In NOPI, the celery root is roasted whole as it is, for 3 hours, brushed with oil and sprinkled with salt. The results are so delicious and so straightforward that I've taken the liberty of adding one more twist in the form of the coriander seeds. The taste is even more wonderful than before. I like to eat it as it is as a starter, cut into wedges and served with a squeeze of lemon or a dollop of crème fraîche, but you can also serve it as a side to a pork chop or steak.

1. Preheat the oven to 375°F.

2. Pierce the celery root with a small sharp knife all over, about 20 times. Place the celery root in a baking dish and rub generously with the oil, coriander seeds, and 2 tsp flaked salt. Roast for 2½–3 hours, basting every 30 minutes until the celery root is soft all the way through and golden brown on the outside.

3. Cut into wedges and serve with a lemon wedge, a sprinkle of salt, and a drizzle of oil.

Aromatic olive oil mash

Serves four as a side

2 lb 2 oz/1kg red-skinned potatoes, peeled and cut into 1¼-inch/3cm pieces

6 thyme sprigs

3 mint sprigs

4 garlic cloves, peeled

1 lemon: finely shave the peel to get 5 strips

salt

7 tbsp/100ml olive oil

black pepper

TOPPING

¼ cup/60ml olive oil

1 garlic clove, minced

2 tsp thyme leaves, finely chopped

about 8 mint leaves, finely chopped (to get 2 tsp)

1 lemon: finely zest to get 1 tsp, then juice to get 1 tbsp

salt and black pepper

Creamy mash is hard to beat, but I often prefer olive oil–based mashes, especially if the centerpiece of the meal is already very rich. Adding aromatics to your cooking water is a great way to jazz up mash. I've used thyme, mint, lemon, and garlic here, but try experimenting with different herbs and spices.

Get ahead by peeling and cutting the potatoes up to 6 hours in advance if you like. Just keep them in a pot of cold water and drain before starting the recipe.

1. Put the potatoes, thyme sprigs, mint sprigs, garlic, lemon strips, and 2 tsp of salt into a large saucepan. Cover with enough boiling water to rise ¾ inch/2cm above the potatoes. Simmer gently for about 25 minutes, or until the potatoes are soft enough to mash.

2. While the potatoes are boiling, make the topping. Put the oil, garlic, thyme leaves, mint leaves, lemon zest, and lemon juice into a small bowl with ⅛ tsp of salt, and a good grind of pepper. Stir to combine, and set aside.

3. Drain the potatoes into a colander set over a large bowl (you'll use some of the cooking water later, so don't throw it all away). Pick out and discard the thyme and mint sprigs, then return the potatoes to the saucepan (along with the garlic and lemon strips). Use a masher to mash the potatoes, adding the oil and about 10 tbsp/140ml of the cooking water slowly as you go, until you get a smooth mash.

4. Transfer the mash to a platter and use the back of a spoon to create divots in the surface. Drizzle the herb and garlic oil topping evenly over it, finish with a good grind of black pepper, and serve.

Pictured on page 132

Sweet potato mash with lime salsa

This is delicious alongside all sorts of things: grilled chops, for example, grilled sausages, pan-fried pork loin, or tofu. I like to keep the skins, brush them very lightly with olive oil, and roast them for about 8 minutes at 425°F, to eat as a chip-like snack.

1. Preheat the oven to 425°F.

2. Rub the sweet potatoes with 1 tbsp of oil and season with ¼ tsp of salt. Place on a parchment-lined baking sheet, cut side down, and roast for 30–35 minutes, until very soft.

3. While the sweet potatoes are roasting, make the salsa. Put the remaining 3 tbsp of oil into a small bowl with the basil, cilantro, garlic, lime zest, lime juice, and a good pinch of salt and stir to combine.

4. Once cool enough to handle, remove the skins from the sweet potatoes. They should slide off easily, but you can scoop the flesh out with a spoon if you prefer. Mash the flesh together with ⅛ tsp of salt and plenty of black pepper until smooth.

5. Transfer to a platter, create divots in the surface, and spoon the salsa evenly over it. Serve hot.

Serves four as a side

2 lb 2 oz/1kg sweet potatoes, unpeeled and cut in half lengthwise

¼ cup/60ml olive oil

salt

¼ cup/5g basil leaves, finely chopped

¼ cup/5g cilantro, finely chopped

½ garlic clove, minced

2 limes: finely zest to get 2 tsp, then juice to get 1 tbsp

black pepper

Pictured on page 133

Spinach and Gorgonzola–stuffed baked potatoes

I love the strong blue cheese here, but use any other cheese that you have around or prefer—it'll work just as well. This is either a meal in itself, to serve two, or works well to serve four, alongside a simple steak and fresh green salad. The walnuts are optional, but they do add a welcome crunch.

If Esme could have had her way, there would have been more recipes for baked potatoes here. With both apologies and thanks to Esme, this is for those that didn't get in and the two winners that did.

Serves two as a main or four as a side

2 large russet potatoes
  (1½ lb/700g)
1½ tbsp unsalted butter
3 tbsp heavy cream
2¼ oz/60g Gorgonzola
salt and black pepper

**7 oz/200g baby spinach
  leaves**
**2 tbsp/20g walnut
  halves,** lightly toasted
  and broken up into
  ½-inch/1cm pieces
  (optional)

1. Preheat the oven to 450°F.

2. Poke the potatoes a few times with a fork and then place them on a parchment-lined baking sheet. Bake for 1 hour or just over, until the flesh is soft all the way through. Remove from the oven and slice the potatoes in half, lengthwise. Scoop the flesh out into a medium bowl, setting the skins aside on the sheet for later. Roughly mash the potato with 1 tbsp/20g of the butter, the cream, Gorgonzola, ½ tsp of salt, and a generous grind of pepper and set aside.

3. Take the remaining ½ tbsp of butter and divide it among the potato cavities. Sprinkle with a generous pinch of salt and return to the oven for 8 minutes, for the skin to become crisp. Remove from the oven and set aside.

4. Place a medium saucepan, halfway filled with salted water, over high heat. Once boiling, add the spinach for about 10–15 seconds, just to wilt. Drain the spinach, squeezing out as much of the water as possible. Stir into the potato flesh, to combine, then spoon the mash back inside the empty skins, piled high. Bake for 15 minutes, until the top of the mash is crisp and browned. Remove from the oven, sprinkle with the walnuts, and serve.

Baked potatoes with egg and tonnato sauce

Serves four

4 large russet potatoes
(3 lb/1.4kg)

1 tbsp olive oil, plus
extra to serve

flaked sea salt

4 large eggs, soft-boiled
(cooked in boiling water
for 6 minutes, then
refreshed under lots of
cold water) and peeled

TONNATO SAUCE

2 large egg yolks

3 tbsp lemon juice

1¼ cups/25g parsley,
roughly chopped

**4¼ oz/120g good-
quality canned tuna
in oil,** drained

2 tbsp/20g baby capers
(or regular capers,
chopped), drained

2 anchovy fillets in oil,
rinsed and patted dry

1 garlic clove, crushed

¾ cup/180ml olive oil

This brings together two of the most simple and comforting dishes: a baked potato and a soft-boiled egg. If you want to make this even more hearty than it is, fold extra tuna into the sauce before spooning it over the potatoes. If you want to get ahead, the tonnato sauce can be made 1 day in advance and kept in the fridge.

1. Preheat the oven to 450°F.

2. Place the potatoes on a baking sheet, drizzle with the oil, sprinkle with ½ tsp salt, and bake for 50–55 minutes, or until the skin is crisp and the middle is soft. Remove from the oven and set aside.

3. While the potatoes are in the oven, make the sauce. Place the egg yolks in the bowl of a food processor with the lemon juice, 1 cup/20g of parsley, the tuna, half the capers, all the anchovies, and the garlic. Blitz for 1 minute to form a rough paste, scraping down the sides of the bowl with a spatula to help the machine. With the machine still running, slowly add the oil in a steady stream, until the consistency is that of a thin mayonnaise. Set aside.

4. When ready to serve, slice the hot potatoes almost (but not completely) in half; leave the base of the skin intact. Squeeze the outside of the potatoes a little—this helps to loosen their flesh—and sprinkle the insides with a pinch of flaked salt. Spoon the sauce over the potatoes and top with an egg, torn in half just before serving so that the yolk runs into the sauce. Add the remaining ¼ cup/5g of parsley and capers, drizzle with some oil, and serve.

Oven fries with oregano and feta

Serves six as a side

4½ lb/2kg yellow potatoes, unpeeled and cut into ¾-inch/2cm-wide fries

6 tbsp/90ml sunflower oil

flaked sea salt

¼ cup/60ml olive oil

6 garlic cloves, thinly sliced

2 tsp dried oregano (regular or Greek)

5¼ oz/150g feta, roughly crumbled

These are inspired by some fries I ate in George Calombaris's Melbourne-based restaurant, Jimmy Grants, when I was in Australia judging on MasterChef. I'd heard great things, but my high expectations were still exceeded. Eat these fries as they are, as a side to some fish or meat and with a simple salad, or with a wedge of lemon to squeeze over them.

If you happen to be on holiday in Greece (or live near a shop that sells Greek produce), be sure to pick up some dried Greek oregano—its flavor is much more intense than regular dried oregano.

Get ahead by parboiling the potatoes up to 6 hours in advance.

1. Preheat the oven to 450°F.

2. Place a large pot filled with plenty of salted water over high heat. Once boiling, add the potatoes and cook for 7–8 minutes, until starting to soften at the edges but still holding their shape. Drain and set aside to dry out for 5 minutes, then transfer to a large bowl. Add the sunflower oil along with 1 tbsp salt and mix well.

3. Tip the potatoes and sunflower oil onto two large parchment-lined baking sheets (so that they are not overcrowded) and bake for 40–50 minutes, stirring a few times, until golden brown and crisp.

4. About 5 minutes before the fries are ready, heat the olive oil and garlic in a small saucepan over medium-high heat. Fry gently for 3–4 minutes, until the garlic is pale golden brown. Take the cooked fries out of the oven and pour the olive oil and garlic over them, then return to the oven for a further 4 minutes. Remove from the oven and, while piping hot, sprinkle with the oregano and feta. Serve at once.

Pictured on page 140

Shallow-fried potatoes with rosemary and sumac

Sumac is a bright and astringent ground spice that I have been championing for a very long time. Its color and kick means it's a great way to shake up all sorts of everyday dishes.

1. Put the oil into a large sauté pan and place over medium heat. Once hot, add the potatoes, garlic and ¾ tsp of salt. Fry gently for 30 minutes, stirring frequently, until the potatoes are golden brown and soft. Add the rosemary and thyme and fry for another 5 minutes, until the herbs are crisp and aromatic.

2. Use a slotted spoon—you want most of the oil to be drained off—to transfer the potatoes and rosemary and thyme to a serving bowl. Stir in the sumac and serve.

Serves four as a side

10 tbsp/150ml olive oil

1 lb 10 oz/750g yellow fingerling potatoes, quartered lengthwise

5 garlic cloves, peeled

salt

3 rosemary sprigs

3 thyme sprigs

2 tsp sumac

Pictured on page 141

Harissa and confit garlic roasted potatoes

Serves six to eight as a side

2 large heads of garlic, cloves peeled (3¼ oz/90g)

½ cup plus 1½ tbsp/ 130g goose or duck fat

4 rosemary sprigs

6 thyme sprigs

4½ lb/2kg yellow potatoes, peeled and cut into 2-inch/5cm chunks

¼ cup/40g ground semolina

2 tsp caraway seeds, toasted and lightly crushed

2 tbsp rose harissa (or 50 percent more or less, depending on variety; see page 301)

flaked sea salt

Any recipe with the word confit *in it is enough to put some people off, but don't be intimidated! All that it entails, in this context, is slow-cooking the garlic for so long that the oil becomes wonderfully infused and the cloves themselves become super soft. The confit garlic can be made up to 2 days in advance and the potatoes can be prepared up to the point of them going in the oven, about 6 hours in advance.*

1. Preheat the oven to 350°F.

2. Place the garlic cloves in a small ovenproof pan or saucepan with a lid, with the goose fat, rosemary, and thyme. Cover and bake for 40 minutes, until the garlic cloves are soft and caramelized. Remove from the oven, then strain the fat into a large heatproof bowl and keep it. Set the garlic and herbs aside.

3. Increase the oven to 425°F.

4. Meanwhile, bring a large pot of salted water to a boil over high heat. Once boiling, add the potatoes and boil for 10 minutes, until the potatoes are half-cooked. Drain well, shaking the potatoes about a bit to fluff up the edges, and set aside in a colander to dry out for about 10 minutes.

5. Add the potatoes to the bowl of goose fat along with the semolina, caraway, harissa, and 2 tsp of salt. Mix together well, then spread out on a large parchment-lined baking sheet. Bake for 45 minutes, until golden brown, turning the potatoes over once or twice throughout. Stir in the confit garlic and herbs and continue to roast for 10–15 minutes, until the potatoes are dark golden brown and crispy. Sprinkle with extra salt, if you like, and serve.

Sweet potato fries

These are lovely either as a side or a snack. If a snack, serve alongside some sour cream, for everyone to dip their fries into. The potatoes can be prepared up to 6 hours in advance, up to the point of placing them in the oven.

1. Preheat the oven to 450°F.

2. Mix the sweet potatoes in a large bowl with the paprika, cayenne, garlic, polenta, oil, and 1 tsp flaked salt. Once combined, tip the sweet potatoes (and all the oil) onto two large parchment-lined baking sheets and roast for 25–30 minutes, stirring gently once or twice, until the potatoes are cooked, crisp and golden brown.

3. Remove from the oven, sprinkle with the sumac and 1 tsp flaked salt, and serve at once.

Serves six to eight as a side

3 very large sweet potatoes, peeled and sliced into ½-inch/ 1½cm-thick fries (2½ lb/1.2kg)

1 tbsp sweet smoked paprika

½ tsp cayenne

3 garlic cloves, minced

3 tbsp polenta

7 tbsp/100ml olive oil

flaked sea salt

1 tbsp sumac

Harissa–baked potato skins and crispy lettuce salad

Serves four to six

2½ lb/1.2kg large russet potatoes
(3 or 4 potatoes)

1 tbsp rose harissa
(or 50 percent more or less, depending on variety; see page 301)

2 tbsp olive oil

salt

1 small iceberg lettuce, trimmed and cut into 1¼-inch/3cm-wide wedges (12¼ oz/350g)

¼ cup/5g tarragon, roughly chopped

DRESSING

2 tbsp preserved lemon peel, thinly sliced (from 2 small preserved lemons)

2 tbsp olive oil

1 lemon: finely zest to get ½ tsp, then juice to get 1 tbsp

1 tsp cumin seeds, toasted and roughly crushed

salt

The basis of this recipe is that you'll be using up skins from potatoes you've already cooked and have sitting around. This is either because you've used the cooked flesh to make mash or, in one of life's great mysteries, your kids have eaten the inside of a baked potato and left the best bit (i.e., the cooked skins)! Either way, don't throw them away—they bring a great extra crunch to an already fresh and crunchy salad and they turn this into a dish you can get onto the table in less than 30 minutes. This is totally brilliant alongside the Slow-cooked chicken with a crisp corn crust (page 236).

All the elements can be made in advance: the dressing up to 3 days and the potato skins can be kept in a sealed container for 1 day at room temperature. Just assemble when ready to serve.

1. Preheat the oven to 450°F.

2. Place the potatoes on a small baking sheet and bake for 50–55 minutes, until soft all the way through. Remove from the oven and, when cool enough to handle, cut in half, scoop out the flesh (don't scrape clean—you want there to be a bit of flesh attached), and set aside for another recipe (see above).

3. Tear the potato skins into 2–2½-inch/5–6cm pieces and place in a medium bowl with the harissa, oil, and ¼ tsp of salt. Mix well, then spread out evenly on a wire rack placed inside a large baking sheet. Bake for 12 minutes, flipping halfway through, until they are dark golden brown and turning crisp. Remove from the oven and set aside to cool and continue to crisp up. Place in a large bowl with the lettuce wedges and tarragon.

4. Whisk together all the ingredients for the dressing with ¼ tsp of salt and pour over the salad. Mix well and serve.

Pictured on page 148

New potatoes with peas and cilantro

This is a lovely side to have with lamb or all sorts of other spring things. If it is spring and you see some sorrel leaves, then add them here, roughly chopped, for an extra burst of flavor. A few chopped anchovies also work well.

This dish can be made a few hours in advance—just warm through before serving.

1. Fill a small saucepan with plenty of water and place over high heat. Bring to a boil, then add the peas and blanch for 1 minute. Drain and set a third of the peas aside. Place the remaining peas in a food processor with the chiles, preserved lemon, ¾ cup of the cilantro, olive oil, lemon zest, a rounded ¼ tsp of salt, and plenty of pepper. Blitz to form a rough paste and set aside.

2. Place a large saucepan filled with plenty of salted water over high heat. Once boiling, add the potatoes and boil for 15 minutes, or until soft. Drain and set aside in a large bowl. Roughly crush—you want at least a third of them left whole. Add the peas—both the blitzed and the whole ones—to the potatoes along with the lemon juice and ¼ cup/5g cilantro leaves. Gently stir and serve warm.

Serves four as a side

2½ cups/300g peas, fresh or frozen

2 green chiles, finely chopped

1 small preserved lemon, seeds discarded (¾ oz/20g)

¾ cup/15g cilantro, roughly chopped, plus an extra ¼ **cup/ 5g leaves** to garnish

¼ cup/60ml olive oil

1 small lemon: finely zest ½ to get ½ tsp, then juice to get 1 tsp

salt and black pepper

1 lb 10 oz/750g new potatoes, sliced in half if large

Pictured on page 149

Pizza bianca with potato, anchovy, and sage

Making your own pizza dough is easy, rolling it out is fun, and it's a great thing to get kids involved with in the kitchen. Make the dough up to 3 days in advance and refrigerate. The potatoes and mascarpone topping can be made the day before.

Makes two pizzas, to serve two as a main with a salad or four as a snack

DOUGH

1 cup plus 6 tbsp/200g
  bread flour, plus extra
  for dusting the worktop

1 tsp fast-acting instant
  dried yeast

1 tbsp olive oil, plus extra
  for greasing

salt

½ cup/120ml lukewarm
  water

TOPPING

6⅓ oz/180g new
  potatoes, unpeeled
  and thinly sliced
  on a mandoline

3 tbsp olive oil

salt and black pepper

¾ cup plus 1½ tbsp/
  200g mascarpone

1½ oz/40g pecorino
  romano, finely grated

4 anchovy fillets, drained
  and finely chopped

8 sage leaves, finely
  chopped

2 lemons: finely zest to
  get 2 tsp

5 green onions, thinly
  sliced at an angle
  (rounded ¾ cup/50g)

1. Put the flour and yeast in a large bowl with the oil and ½ tsp salt. Stir to combine, then pour in the water, using a spatula to bring together. Transfer to a lightly oiled surface, then, with lightly oiled hands, knead the dough for 5 minutes until soft and elastic. Add more oil if it starts to stick. Divide

the dough in half and transfer to a large parchment-lined baking sheet, spaced well apart. Cover with a slightly damp kitchen towel and let rise in a warm place for 60–90 minutes, to double in size.

2. Preheat the oven to 475°F or as high as it goes.

3. While the dough is rising, make the topping. In a small bowl, combine the potatoes with 1 tbsp of oil, ⅛ tsp of salt, and a good grind of pepper. Transfer the potato slices to a parchment-lined baking sheet, big enough that the slices can lie flat and be spaced apart. Roast for 7 minutes, until golden brown, then set aside.

4. In a small bowl, combine the mascarpone, pecorino, anchovies, sage, and lemon zest with a good grind of pepper and set aside.

5. Grease two large baking sheets with olive oil. Lightly flour your work surface. Working with one piece at a time, roll the dough into a rectangle that's 12 x 8 inches/30 x 20cm. Carefully transfer to the baking sheet and repeat with the second ball of dough. Spread the mascarpone mixture evenly over both dough bases, leaving a ¾ inch/2cm uncovered border around the edge. Sprinkle the green onions on top, then layer on the potatoes. Drizzle each pizza with about 1 tbsp of oil and bake for 9 minutes, until the edges are crisp and golden. Serve warm with a good grind of black pepper.

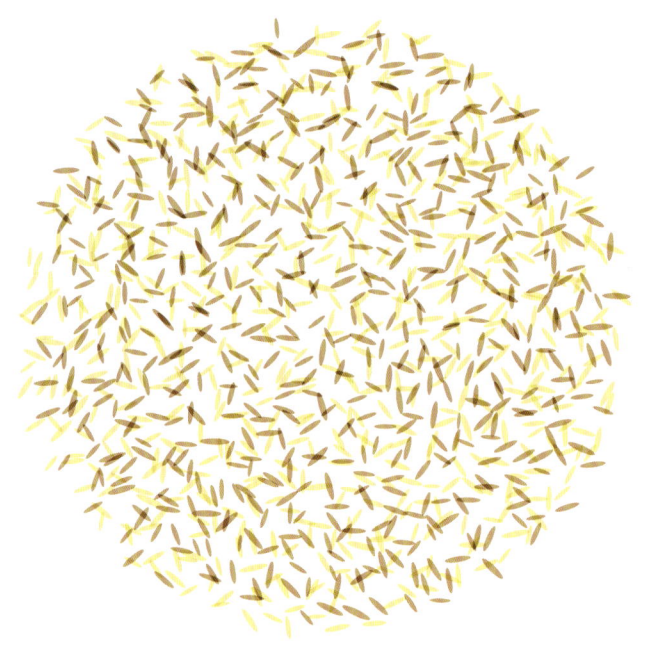

Rice, Grains, and Pulses

Buckwheat and haricots verts salad

This is either lovely as it is or served with some pan-fried salmon. It's quick to make—less than half an hour if you get the various elements all cooking at the same time—but can also be prepared in advance, if you like. All the elements can be made 1 day ahead and kept separately in the fridge, ready for the dish to be assembled before serving.

1. Preheat the oven to 425°F.

2. Mix the onions in a large bowl with 1 tbsp of oil and ⅛ tsp of salt. Spread out on a large parchment-lined baking sheet and roast for 18–20 minutes, until cooked through and golden. Remove from the oven and set aside to cool.

3. Bring a medium saucepan with slightly salted water to a boil. Add the buckwheat and cook for 8 minutes. Add the green beans and cook for 5 minutes, until both the green beans and buckwheat are al dente. Drain, refresh under cold water, and then set aside to dry well.

4. Mix together all the ingredients for the sauce with ⅛ tsp of salt in a bowl and set aside.

5. When ready to serve, mix the onions, buckwheat, green beans, mint, and tarragon with the remaining 1 tbsp of oil and ½ tsp of salt. Transfer the salad to a serving bowl and serve the sauce on the side or swirl the sauce through the salad before transferring it to the serving bowl. Sprinkle with the chile flakes and serve.

Serves four

2 small red onions, peeled and cut into ¾-inch/2cm wedges (3 cups/300g)

2 tbsp olive oil

salt

½ cup/90g buckwheat groats

12¼ oz/350g haricots verts, trimmed and cut in half

¼ cup/5g mint leaves, roughly chopped

¼ cup/5g tarragon leaves, roughly chopped

1 tsp Urfa chile flakes (or ½ tsp other crushed red pepper flakes), to serve

SAUCE

6 tbsp/100g Greek-style yogurt

1 small garlic clove, minced

1 tbsp olive oil

2 tsp lemon juice

¼ tsp dried mint

Couscous, cherry tomato, and herb salad

Serves four

1½ cups/250g couscous

6 tbsp/90ml olive oil

2 tsp ras el hanout

salt and black pepper

1⅔ cups/400ml boiling water

10 oz/300g cherry tomatoes

2 onions, sliced paper-thin (3 cups/300g)

¼ cup/30g golden raisins

1 tsp cumin seeds, toasted and lightly crushed

⅓ cup/50g roasted and salted almonds, roughly chopped

¾ cup/15g cilantro leaves, roughly chopped

¾ cup/15g mint leaves, roughly torn

1 lemon: finely zest to get 1 tsp, then juice to get 1 tbsp

This salad is perfect at a summer barbecue, great alongside all sorts of grilled meats and grilled vegetables. Make the couscous, onion, and raisin mix 1 day in advance, if you like, and keep separately in the fridge—just bring back to room temperature before serving.

1. Place the couscous in a medium bowl. Drizzle with 2 tbsp of oil, sprinkle with 1 tsp of ras el hanout, ¾ tsp of salt, and plenty of pepper, then pour in the boiling water. Stir, cover the bowl tightly with foil and set aside for 20 minutes. Remove the foil, fluff the couscous with a fork, and set aside to cool.

2. Put 1 tbsp of oil into a large frying pan and place over high heat. Once hot, add the tomatoes and fry for 3–4 minutes, stirring a few times, until they start to brown and split open. Remove from the pan, sprinkle with a pinch of salt, and set aside with any juices.

3. Wipe the pan clean, then add the remaining 3 tbsp of oil and return to medium-high heat. Add the onions, the remaining 1 tsp of ras el hanout, and ⅛ tsp salt and fry for 10–12 minutes, stirring, until dark golden brown and soft. Remove from the heat, stir in the raisins, and set aside to cool.

4. Once the couscous has cooled slightly, transfer it to a large bowl. Add the onion and raisin mix and stir. Add the cumin, almonds, cilantro, mint, lemon zest, lemon juice, ¼ tsp salt, and a generous grind of pepper and mix gently.

5. Transfer to a serving platter, top with the tomatoes, and serve.

 Pictured on page 160

Puy lentil and eggplant stew

Few things bring me more pleasure in the kitchen than taking a set of familiar ingredients and seeing them in a new light. It's happened here with this stew and the Puy lentil and eggplant dish on page 166. The two ingredient lists are very similar—the eggplant, cherry tomatoes, olive oil, garlic, and oregano. Both dishes, though equally delicious, are completely different from one another. It's one of the many reasons I love eggplants—they're so versatile and can be cooked in such different ways to yield such different results.

Serve the stew either as a hearty starter or a side, or else as a main, served with any grain you like. The stew can be made up to 3 days ahead and kept in the fridge—just warm through and add the crème fraîche, oil, chile flakes, and oregano before serving.

1. Put 2 tbsp of oil into a large high-sided sauté pan and place over medium-high heat. Add the garlic, onion, thyme, and ¼ tsp salt and fry for 8 minutes, stirring often, until soft and golden. Tip into a bowl, leaving the oil behind. Set aside.

2. Place the eggplant and tomatoes in a bowl and season with ¼ tsp of salt and plenty of pepper. Add the remaining 1 tbsp of oil to the same pan (don't worry about wiping it clean) and, once very hot, add the eggplant and tomatoes. Fry for 10 minutes, over medium-high, turning them often until the eggplant is soft and golden brown and the tomatoes are beginning to blacken. Return the garlic and onion to the pan, then add the lentils, stock, wine, water, and ¾ tsp salt. Bring to a boil. Decrease the heat to medium and simmer gently for about 40 minutes, until the lentils are soft but still retain a bite.

3. Serve warm or at room temperature, with dollops of crème fraîche, a drizzle of oil, and chile flakes and oregano on top.

Serves four as a starter
or two as a main

3 tbsp olive oil, plus
    extra to serve
3 garlic cloves,
    thinly sliced
1 large red onion,
    finely chopped
    (1 cup/160g)
1½ tsp thyme leaves
salt
2 small eggplants,
    cut into chunks, about
    2 x ¾ inch/5 x 2cm
    (6 cups/420g)
7 oz/200g cherry
    tomatoes
black pepper
¾ cup plus 2 tbsp/
    180g Puy lentils
2 cups/500ml vegetable
    stock
⅓ cup/80ml dry white
    wine
1¾ cups/450ml water
6 tbsp/100g crème
    fraîche
1 tsp Urfa chile flakes
    (or ½ tsp other crushed
    red pepper flakes)
2 tsp oregano leaves

Pictured on page 161

Bulgur with tomato, eggplant, and lemon yogurt

Serves four as a main
or eight as a side

2 small eggplants, cut
  into 1¼-inch/3cm
  chunks (6 cups/500g)

7 tbsp plus 1 tsp/
  105ml olive oil

salt and black pepper

2 onions, thinly sliced
  (3 cups/320g)

3 garlic cloves, minced

1 tsp ground allspice

14 oz/400g cherry
  tomatoes

1 tbsp tomato paste

1⅔ cups/400ml water

1½ cups/250g bulgur
  wheat

⅔ cup/200g Greek-style
  yogurt

1 small preserved
  lemon, seeds
  discarded, skin and
  flesh finely chopped
  (2 tbsp/25g)

½ cup/10g mint leaves,
  finely shredded

You can make just the bulgur and tomato, if you like (without the eggplant and preserved lemon yogurt) and serve it as a side. With the eggplant and yogurt, though, it makes a satisfying vegetarian main. You can make all the elements up to 1 day ahead—just keep separate in the fridge, warm through and assemble before serving.

1. Preheat the oven to 425°F.

2. Place the eggplant in a large bowl with 4 tbsp of the oil, ½ tsp salt, and a good grind of pepper. Mix well and then spread out on a large parchment-lined baking sheet. Roast for 35–40 minutes, stirring halfway through, until the eggplant is caramelized and soft. Remove from the oven and set aside.

3. Add the remaining 3 tbsp plus 1 tsp of oil to a large sauté pan with a lid and place over medium-high heat. Once hot, add the onions and fry for 8 minutes, stirring a few times, until caramelized and soft. Add the garlic and allspice and fry for 1 minute, stirring continuously, until the garlic is aromatic and starting to brown. Add the cherry tomatoes, mashing them with a potato masher to break them up. Stir in the tomato paste, water, and 1 tsp salt. Bring to a boil, decrease the heat to medium-low, cover, and cook for 12 minutes. Add the bulgur, stir so that it is completely coated, and then remove from the heat. Set aside for 20 minutes, for the bulgur to absorb all the liquid.

4. In a medium bowl, mix together the yogurt with the preserved lemon, half the mint, and ⅛ tsp salt.

5. Divide the bulgur among four plates. Serve with the yogurt and eggplant on top and a sprinkle of the remaining mint.

Bulgur with mushrooms and feta

This works as both a side and a main, with some wilted greens alongside. Get as diverse a mix of mushrooms as you can and like. Thanks to food writer Limor Laniado Tiroche, writing in Haaretz, *who inspired this dish.*

Serves four as a side or two as a main

¾ **cup plus 2 tbsp/ 150g bulgur wheat**

salt and black pepper

I cup plus I tbsp/ 250ml boiling water

¼ **cup plus I tsp/65ml olive oil,** plus extra to serve

I large onion, thinly sliced (1⅔ cups/170g)

I tsp cumin seeds

I lb 2 oz/500g mixed mushrooms, thinly sliced (or torn apart if wild)

2 tbsp thyme leaves

2 tbsp balsamic vinegar

½ **cup/10g dill,** roughly chopped, plus extra to serve

2¼ **oz/60g feta,** broken into ½–¾ inch/1–2cm pieces

I tsp Urfa chile flakes (or ½ tsp other crushed red pepper flakes)

1. Rinse the bulgur and place in a large bowl. Stir in ¼ tsp of salt and a good grind of pepper, then pour in the boiling water. Cover the bowl with plastic wrap and set aside for 20 minutes, until the liquid has been absorbed and the bulgur is soft. Drain, if there is any liquid left, and set aside.

2. Meanwhile, put 2 tbsp of oil into a large sauté pan and place over medium-high heat. Add the onion and fry for 7–8 minutes, until soft and caramelized. Add ½ tsp of the cumin and continue to fry for 1–2 minutes, until dark golden brown. Remove from the pan and set aside.

3. Add the remaining 2 tbsp plus 1 tsp of oil to the same pan and increase the heat to high. Mix in the mushrooms and ½ tsp of salt and fry for 6–7 minutes, stirring frequently, until the mushrooms have browned and softened. Add the remaining ½ tsp of cumin and the thyme and continue to cook for 1 minute, stirring continuously. Pour in the balsamic vinegar and continue to cook for about 30 seconds—it should reduce to practically nothing. Stir in the bulgur, onion, dill, feta, and chile flakes, until warmed through, then remove from the heat.

4. Spoon the bulgur and mushrooms onto a large platter or two individual plates. Sprinkle some extra dill over the top, drizzle with oil, and serve.

Puy lentils with eggplant, tomatoes, and yogurt

For the sake of ease, I've roasted the eggplant here in a hot oven. If you want to really get a smoky taste into the flesh of the eggplant, though, it's best to put it directly on the open flame on your stove. I line my stove top with foil when doing this (making holes for the flames to come through), then use long tongs to help turn the eggplant so that all sides get burnt. This method can be a bit messy, but the upside is that it takes just 15–20 minutes, rather than 1 hour, and the resulting smoky taste is more intense.

This can be made up to 3 days in advance, up to the point of the yogurt being added. Keep in the fridge until needed.

Serves four as a starter or side or two as a main

4 eggplants, pricked a few times with a knife (2 lb 6 oz/1.1 kg)

10 oz/300g cherry tomatoes

¾ cup/160g Puy lentils (or 4⅔ cups/350g ready-cooked lentils, if you want to save time)

2 tbsp olive oil, plus extra to serve

1½ tbsp lemon juice

1 small garlic clove, minced

3 tbsp oregano leaves

salt and black pepper

6 tbsp/100g Greek-style yogurt

1. Preheat the oven to 475°F or as high as your oven will go.

2. Place the eggplants on a baking sheet and roast for 1 hour, turning them over halfway through, until the flesh is completely soft and slightly smoky. Remove from the oven and, once cool enough handle, scoop the flesh out into a colander. Set aside, in the sink or over a bowl, for 30 minutes, for any liquid to drain away. The skin can be discarded.

3. Place the cherry tomatoes on the same baking sheet and roast for 12 minutes, until slightly blackened, split, and soft. Remove from the oven and set aside.

4. Meanwhile, if starting with uncooked lentils, fill a medium saucepan with plenty of water and place over high heat. Once boiling, add the lentils, decrease the heat to medium, and cook for 20 minutes, until soft but still retaining a bite. Drain, then set aside to dry out slightly. If starting with ready-cooked lentils, just tip them into a large bowl and add the eggplant flesh, tomatoes, oil, lemon juice, garlic, 2 tbsp of oregano, ¾ tsp salt, and a good grind of pepper. Mix well, then spoon into a large shallow bowl. Top with the yogurt, swirling it through slightly so there are obvious streaks. Sprinkle the remaining 1 tbsp of oregano over the top, drizzle with a little oil, and serve.

Brown rice with caramelized onions and black garlic

Serves four as a side

¼ **cup plus 1 tsp/65ml sunflower oil**

2 **large onions,** cut into ¾-inch/2cm wedges (5 cups/500g)

salt

1 **lemon:** peel finely shaved, plus 2 tbsp juice

1 **cup/200g brown rice,** rinsed

2 **cups/500ml water**

10 **black garlic cloves,** thinly sliced

½ **cup/150g Greek-style yogurt**

½ **cup/10g parsley leaves,** roughly chopped

This rich rice dish is a lovely accompaniment to lamb or pork, but also works well as it is, with a plate of fresh or steamed veg. It's also a great introduction to black garlic if you've yet to shake hands. The balsamic-licorice flavor and squidgy texture of the cloves makes them easy to slice or blitz, and they're an even easier way to add a ton of flavor to all sorts of dishes. Don't be afraid to really caramelize the onions—the darker the color, the sweeter the flavor. The onions can be made the day before you need them and kept in the fridge.

1. Pour 3 tbsp/50ml of oil into a large sauté pan with a lid, and place over medium-high heat. Once hot, add the onions, along with ¼ tsp salt, and fry for 12 minutes, stirring occasionally to make sure they don't burn. Add the lemon peel and cook for another 12 minutes, continuing to stir from time to time, until the onions are dark and caramelized. Transfer to a plate and set aside.

2. Add the remaining 1 tbsp plus 1 tsp of oil to the pan, then add the rice and ½ tsp of salt. Fry for 1 minute, stirring continuously, then pour in the water. Bring to a boil, then decrease the heat to medium-low. Cover the pan and simmer for about 45 minutes, until cooked through. Remove from the heat and stir in the onions, lemon juice, and black garlic. Serve at once, topping each serving with a generous spoonful of the yogurt and a sprinkle of parsley; alternatively, you can serve the yogurt in a bowl on the side.

Baked mint rice with pomegranate and olive salsa

Cooking rice perfectly is one of those things that shouldn't be complicated but can be surprisingly difficult, for some, to get right. Baking it in the oven, on the other hand, as I do here, is a completely foolproof method (and one that worked, incidentally, when feeding 700 people during two sittings at Wilderness Festival in 2017!). This is such a great side to all sorts of dishes, such as roasted root vegetables or slow-cooked lamb or pork.

To get ahead, the salsa can be made a few hours in advance and kept in the fridge.

1. Preheat the oven to 475°F, or as high as your oven will go.

2. Place the rice in a high-sided ovenproof dish, measuring 8 x 12 inches/20 x 30cm. Season with ¾ tsp of salt and plenty of pepper, then pour in the butter and boiling water. Top with the sprigs of mint and cover the dish tightly with foil so that the rice is well sealed. Bake for 25 minutes, until the rice is light and fluffy and all the liquid has been absorbed.

3. Meanwhile, make the salsa: place the olives, pomegranate, walnuts, olive oil, pomegranate molasses, garlic, mint, and salt in a medium bowl. Mix well and set aside.

4. Take the rice out of the oven and remove and discard the foil. Pull the leaves off the mint sprigs—the stalks can be discarded—then place these back on the rice and sprinkle with the feta. Just before serving, spoon the salsa evenly over the rice. Serve hot.

Serves six

2 cups/400g basmati rice

salt and black pepper

¼ cup/50g unsalted butter, melted

3⅓ cups/800ml boiling water

1½ oz/40g mint sprigs

SALSA

⅓ cup/40g pitted green olives, thinly sliced

seeds from 1 small pomegranate
(⅔ cup/90g)

½ cup/50g walnut halves, lightly roasted and roughly broken

3 tbsp olive oil

1 tbsp pomegranate molasses

1 small garlic clove, minced

½ cup/10g mint leaves

¼ tsp salt

5¼ oz/150g feta, crumbled into ½–¾ inch/1–2cm pieces

Thai sticky rice with crispy ginger, chile, and peanuts

Sticky rice is brilliant as it is, served alongside all sorts of fish and meat dishes, but the addition of a crispy topping makes it even more wonderful. I like to serve this with the whole roasted sea bass (page 260) or fried tofu, as part of an Asian-style feast. Get all your chopping done before you start here—you want everything to be ready to chuck into the pan when it's hot, rather than slicing things into matchsticks at this stage.

1. Put the rice into a medium saucepan with a well-fitting lid, along with ½ tsp salt and the water. Bring to a boil, then decrease the heat to medium-low and simmer gently, covered, for 15 minutes. Remove from the heat and set aside, still covered, for 5 minutes.

2. While the rice is cooking, put the oil into a medium frying pan and place over medium-high heat. Once hot, add the ginger, garlic and chiles and fry for 3–4 minutes, stirring frequently, until just starting to brown. Add the cilantro, peanuts, sesame seeds, and a generous pinch of salt and continue to fry for 1–2 minutes, until golden brown. Spoon over the rice and serve, with the wedges of lime alongside.

Serves six as a side
2 cups/400g Thai sticky rice
salt
2½ cups/600ml water
1½ tbsp peanut oil
2-inch/5cm piece of ginger, peeled and julienned (5 tbsp/40g)
3 garlic cloves, thinly sliced
2 red chiles, julienned
1½ cups/30g cilantro stems, cut into 1¼-inch/3cm lengths
3 tbsp salted and roasted peanuts, roughly chopped
1 tbsp sesame seeds
1 lime, cut into 6 wedges, to serve

Baked rice with confit tomatoes and garlic

Serves six as a side or four as a main

1¾ lb/800g cherry tomatoes

12 large garlic cloves (or 25 small), peeled (⅔ cup/85g)

4 large shallots, cut into 1¼-inch/3cm pieces (1 cup/220g)

1¼ cups/25g cilantro stems, cut into 1½-inch/4cm lengths, plus **½ cup/10g leaves,** roughly chopped, to serve

3 tbsp thyme leaves

4 small cinnamon sticks

7 tbsp/100ml olive oil

salt and black pepper

1½ cups/300g basmati rice

2½ cups/600ml boiling water

This was my go-to side for a good few months, working well with pretty much anything else on the table. There's also enough going on, flavorwise, for it to be lovely as it is, as a main.

Peeling so many garlic cloves won't win me any "simple" brownie points, I know, but, once done, the simple joy of this dish is that the rice is baked in the oven rather than on the stove. For those who find creating perfectly cooked rice in a pan of simmering water strangely difficult, this will be a revelation. Just make sure the foil is sealed tightly over the dish—you don't want any steam to escape in the oven.

1. Preheat the oven to 350°F.

2. Arrange the tomatoes, garlic, shallots, cilantro stems, thyme, and cinnamon sticks in a large high-sided casserole dish, about 8 x 12 inches/20 x 30cm. Pour in the olive oil, add ½ tsp of salt and a good grind of black pepper, and place in the oven for 1 hour, until the vegetables are soft. Remove from the oven, sprinkle the rice evenly over the vegetables, without stirring them together, and set aside.

3. Increase the oven temperature to 450°F.

4. Sprinkle ½ tsp of salt and plenty of black pepper over the rice and then carefully pour the boiling water over the rice. Seal the dish tightly with foil and place in the oven for 25 minutes, until the rice is cooked. Remove from the oven and set aside for 10 minutes, still covered. Remove the foil, sprinkle with the cilantro leaves, stir these very gently into the rice, and serve.

Noodles
and Pasta

Rice noodle salad with cucumber and poppy seeds

Serves six to eight

¼ **cup/60ml apple cider vinegar**

2½ **tbsp/30g sugar**

I small red onion, thinly sliced (mounded I cup/120g)

2-inch/5cm piece of ginger, peeled and julienned (5 tbsp/40g)

5¼ **oz/150g flat rice noodles,** broken into roughly 6-inch/15cm pieces

3 tbsp olive oil

I Granny Smith apple, cored and sliced into ¹⁄₁₆-inch/2mm-thick pieces (¾ cup/120g)

I large English cucumber, unpeeled, halved lengthwise, seeds scooped out, and flesh cut into long, thin strips (2½ cups/250g)

2 red chiles, seeded and julienned

¾ **cup/15g mint leaves,** torn or roughly chopped

¾ **cup/15g tarragon,** torn or roughly chopped

I tbsp poppy seeds

salt

For anyone who thinks that this list of ingredients looks suspiciously long for a book of simple recipes, I'm actually feeling quite pleased with how I've managed to get the list down. My ability to buy up half the stock in an Asian shop when making noodle salads has been well documented in letters from some of my readers over the years, written to the Guardian.

All the elements can be made a few hours in advance—the onion and ginger can be made the day before—and just assembled when ready to serve.

1. Whisk together the vinegar and sugar in a medium bowl until the sugar has dissolved. Add the onion and ginger and stir to coat. Set aside for about 30 minutes, stirring a few times, to soften.

2. Place the noodles in a large bowl and pour over enough boiling water to cover them. Set aside for 15–20 minutes, until the noodles are soft, then drain well. Mix with 1 tbsp of oil and set aside in a large bowl to cool down.

3. Add the apple, cucumber, chiles, mint, tarragon, and poppy seeds to the noodles, plus the pickled onion, ginger and juices, the remaining 2 tbsp of oil, and 1½ tsp salt. Mix together well and serve at once.

Soba noodles with lime, cardamom, and avocado

Scraping the seeds from 12 cardamom pods and crushing them might feel like a bit of a fiddle, just for ½ tsp, but it's a few minutes well worth spending. Unleashing the fruity, floral, and citrusy spice into the dish makes it really quite distinct.

I like to eat this either as it is, for a quick lunch or light supper, or with some shrimp or tofu stirred in just before serving. It also works well served alongside some pan-fried salmon or topped with a soft-boiled egg.

1. Cook the noodles according to the instructions on the package (they vary from brand to brand). Once cooked, refresh under cold running water and set aside in a colander to drain well.

2. With the flat side of a knife, crush the cardamom pods to open them up. Scrape the seeds out into a pestle and mortar and discard the outer husks. Crush the seeds—you should get about ½ tsp—and place in a large bowl with the noodles. Add the basil, cilantro, pistachios, lime zest, lime juice, oil, chile, avocado, and ½ tsp salt. Mix everything together well, then divide among four bowls. Spoon any avocado, nuts, and herbs left in the bowl on top. Sprinkle with the nigella seeds and serve with a wedge of lime alongside.

Serves four

7 oz/200g buckwheat noodles (or green tea soba)

12 green cardamom pods

1 ½ cups/30g basil leaves, roughly chopped

1 ½ cups/30g cilantro leaves, roughly chopped

½ cup/70g shelled pistachios, roughly chopped

3 limes: finely zest 2 to get 1 tsp, then juice 2 to get 3 tbsp; slice the final lime into 4 wedges, to serve

3 tbsp peanut oil

1 green chile, seeded and thinly sliced

2 ripe avocados, cut into ¼-inch/½cm slices

salt

¼ tsp nigella seeds or Urfa chile flakes, to sprinkle (optional)

Seaweed spaghetti and sesame salad with tahini dressing

Seaweed spaghetti has a similar texture to rice noodles but brings with it a salty kick. Nanami togarashi is an Asian chile condiment that works really well here, but regular chile flakes are a good alternative.

This is lovely as it is, for a light lunch or starter, or served alongside some sticky rice to bulk it out. It also works well with oily fish—pan-fried mackerel or salmon—or grilled shrimp.

Serve this as soon as you've mixed it together. The cucumber will make it watery if it sits around for too long. The dressing can be made up to 2 days in advance.

1. To make the dressing, put the honey, vinegar, mirin, mustard, soy sauce, tahini, and peanut oil in a small bowl, whisk well to combine, then set aside.

2. Put the seaweed spaghetti into a medium saucepan and cover with cold water. Bring to a boil, then decrease to a simmer and cook for 15 minutes, until al dente. Drain, refresh under cold running water, pat dry, and set aside. Place in a large bowl, along with the cucumber, sesame seeds, cilantro, dressing, and ½ tsp of salt. Mix together, then divide among the bowls (or arrange in a large serving bowl), sprinkle with chile flakes and serve at once.

Serves four

TAHINI DRESSING

1 tsp honey

1½ tsp rice vinegar

1 tbsp mirin

1 tsp Dijon mustard

1½ tsp soy sauce

1 tbsp tahini

1 tbsp peanut oil

1¾ oz/50g seaweed spaghetti

1 large English cucumber, halved lengthwise, seeds scooped out, and flesh cut into long, thin strips (2½ cups/250g)

2 tbsp/20g white or black sesame seeds, or a mixture of both, lightly toasted

¾ cup/15g cilantro leaves

salt

½ tsp crushed red pepper flakes (or nanami togarashi, if you have it)

Pasta alla Norma

After a day in the test kitchen, eating all day, there are just a handful of dishes I'm happy to cook and eat once I get home. This is one of them. If you're getting organized and into batch cooking, double or triple the recipe for the tomato sauce so that this is all ready to go. It keeps in the fridge for 5 days and also freezes well. The eggplant, once roasted, is also happy to sit around (either at room temperature or in the fridge) for 1 day, if you want to get ahead with this too.

If you see any ricotta salata, do get it to try instead of the pecorino romano. It's a variation of ricotta that has been pressed, salted, and dried—its flavor is both salty and nutty. It's firmer than standard ricotta and works really well shaved over spaghetti.

Serves four

3 eggplants (2 lb/900g)

½ cup/120ml olive oil

salt and black pepper

5 garlic cloves, thinly
  sliced

1–2 mild dried chiles
  (seeded if you don't
  want the heat)

2 (14.5 oz/400g) cans
  whole peeled
  plum tomatoes
  with their juice

5 large oregano sprigs

1 tsp sugar

10 oz/300g spaghetti

1½ oz/45g mature
  pecorino romano
  (or ricotta salata),
  shaved

1 cup/20g basil
  leaves, torn

1. Preheat the oven to 450°F.

2. Using a peeler and working from top to bottom of each eggplant, shave off long alternating strips of peel so that they look striped, like zebras. Cut crosswise into ½-inch/1cm slices and place in a bowl with 5 tbsp/75ml of oil, ¾ tsp salt, and a generous grind of pepper. Mix well, then spread out on two large parchment-lined baking sheets. Roast for 30–35 minutes, until dark golden brown. Remove from the oven and set aside to cool.

3. Put 2 tbsp of oil into a sauté pan and place over medium-high heat. Add the garlic and chiles and fry for 1–2 minutes, stirring constantly, until the garlic is golden brown. Add the tomatoes and their juice, oregano, sugar, ½ tsp salt, and a grind of pepper. Decrease the heat to medium-low and cook for 10 minutes, until the sauce is thick. Remove the oregano sprigs and stir in the eggplant. Set aside.

4. Bring a large pot of salted water to a boil and add the spaghetti. Cook until al dente, then strain, reserving some cooking water. Add the spaghetti to the sauce and mix well, adding two-thirds of the pecorino and basil, and a few tbsp of the cooking water if the sauce has become too thick.

5. Divide the spaghetti among four shallow bowls, then top with the remaining pecorino, basil, and 1 tbsp of oil, and serve.

Fettuccine with spiced cherry tomato sauce

Buy a big batch of cherry tomatoes when they are ripe and sweet, and double or triple the quantity of sauce. It takes a while to cook—just over an hour—but it keeps in the fridge for 5 days and freezes for up to 1 month. The ancho chile adds a lovely smoky richness, but can be replaced by ¼ tsp sweet smoked paprika, if you have this on hand rather than ancho. Alternatively, if you don't want the kick, leave the chile out altogether.

1. Put the oil into a large sauté pan and place over medium-high heat. Once hot, add the garlic and fry for up to 1 minute, stirring a few times, until starting to caramelize. Add the tomatoes—carefully, so that the oil doesn't spit—along with the sugar, chile, and ½ tsp of salt. Pour in the water and stir for 4 minutes, until the tomatoes are starting to break down and the liquid is bubbling. Decrease the heat to medium-low and cook for about 1 hour, stirring every once in a while, until the tomatoes and ancho have broken down and the sauce has thickened. Stir in the basil and set aside somewhere warm.

2. Fill a large pot with plenty of salted water and place over high heat. Bring to a boil, then add the pasta. Cook for 10–12 minutes, or according to the package instructions, until al dente. Drain the pasta and stir it into the sauce. Divide among 4 bowls, sprinkle with Parmesan, and serve.

Serves four

5 tbsp/75ml olive oil

2 garlic cloves, thinly sliced

2 lb 2 oz/1kg cherry tomatoes, halved

½ tsp sugar (or a bit more or less, depending on the sweetness of the tomatoes)

1 dried ancho chile, torn apart

salt

¾ cup plus 2 tbsp/200ml water

1 cup/20g basil leaves

14 oz/400g fettuccine (or spaghetti)

1¼ oz/35g Parmesan, finely grated

Pappardelle with rose harissa, black olives, and capers

Serves four

2 tbsp olive oil

1 large onion, thinly
sliced (mounded
2 cups/220g)

3 tbsp rose harissa
(or 50 percent more
or less, depending on
variety; see page 301)

**14 oz/400g cherry
tomatoes,** halved

**½ cup/55g pitted
kalamata olives,** torn
in half

2 tbsp baby capers

salt

**¾ cup plus 2 tbsp/
200ml water**

¾ cup/15g parsley,
roughly chopped

**1 lb 2 oz/500g dried
pappardelle pasta**
(or other wide flat pasta)

**½ cup/120g Greek-style
yogurt**

Pappare means "to gobble up," in Italian, which is the destiny of this dish (particularly in Tara's house, where her husband, Chris, makes it most Sunday nights). I like it spicy, but the quantity of harissa can easily be reduced. Make the sauce 3 days ahead if you like and keep in the fridge until needed.

1. Put the oil into a large sauté pan with a lid and place over medium-high heat. Once hot, add the onion and fry for 8 minutes, stirring every once in a while, until soft and caramelized. Add the harissa, tomatoes, olives, capers, and ½ tsp salt and continue to fry for 3–4 minutes, stirring frequently, until the tomatoes start to break down. Add the water and stir to mix thoroughly. Once boiling, decrease the heat to medium-low, cover the pan, and simmer for 10 minutes. Remove the lid and continue to cook for 4–5 minutes, until the sauce is thick and rich. Stir in ½ cup/10g of the parsley and set aside.

2. Meanwhile, fill a large pot with plenty of salted water and place over high heat. Once boiling, add the pappardelle and cook according to the package instructions, until al dente. Drain well.

3. Return the pasta to the pot along with the harissa sauce and ⅛ tsp of salt. Mix together well, then divide among 4 shallow bowls. Serve hot, with a spoonful of yogurt and a final sprinkle of parsley.

Pictured right with Gigli with chickpeas and za'atar (page 191)

Gigli with chickpeas and za'atar

Gigli *means "lilies" in Italian, and their floral wavy edges are a great vehicle for the chickpeas and anchovies in the sauce. Orecchiette (ears) or conchiglie (shells) are also good for scooping and work really well here too.*

1. Put the olive oil into a large sauté pan and place over high heat. Add the onion, garlic, cumin, thyme, anchovies, lemon peel, ½ tsp of salt, and a good grind of pepper. Fry for 3–4 minutes, stirring often, until soft and golden. Decrease the heat to medium-high, then add the chickpeas and sugar and fry for 8 minutes, stirring occasionally, until the chickpeas begin to brown and crisp up. Add the chicken stock and lemon juice and simmer for 6 minutes, until the sauce has reduced slightly. Remove from the heat and set aside. You can make this in advance, if you like, and warm through before serving.

2. Bring a large pot of salted water to a boil. Add the pasta and cook for 8 minutes, or according to the package instructions, until al dente. Drain and set aside.

3. Stir the spinach and parsley into the chickpeas; the residual heat of the sauce should cook the spinach, but if it doesn't wilt, just warm the chickpeas gently on the stove. Transfer the pasta to the pan of chickpeas and stir to combine. Divide among 4 bowls and sprinkle the za'atar on top. Finish with a drizzle of oil, and serve.

Serves four

3 tbsp olive oil, plus extra to serve

½ **onion,** finely chopped (¾ cup/100g)

2 garlic cloves, minced

2 tsp ground cumin

½ **cup/10g thyme leaves,** finely chopped

about 7 anchovy fillets in oil, drained and finely chopped (scant 1 oz/25g)

1 lemon: finely shave the peel of ½, then juice to get 2 tbsp

salt and black pepper

2 (15.5 oz/440g) cans chickpeas, drained and rinsed (3½ cups/480g)

1 tsp brown sugar

1⅔ **cups/400ml chicken stock**

7 oz/200g gigli pasta (or conchiglie or orecchiette)

1¾ **oz/50g baby spinach leaves**

¾ **cup/15g parsley,** roughly chopped

1½ **tsp za'atar**

Orzo with shrimp, tomato, and marinated feta

The combination of shrimp, feta, tomatoes, and pasta is one that I love. I return to it time and again for easy one-pot suppers. Orzo is the little pasta that comes in the shape of rice. It's easy to eat a lot of and widely available. If you buy shrimp in their shell, then keep a few heads on, just for the look. The marinated feta is lovely dotted over salads, so I tend to make a batch to keep in the fridge for up to 1 week.

1. In a medium bowl, mix the feta with ¼ tsp of the chile flakes, 2 tsp of the fennel seeds, and 1 tbsp of the oil. Set aside while you cook the orzo.

2. Place a large sauté pan with a lid over medium-high heat. Add 2 tbsp of oil, the orzo, ⅛ tsp salt, and a good grind of pepper. Fry for 3–4 minutes, stirring frequently, until golden brown, then remove from the pan and set aside.

3. Return the pan to the medium-high heat and add the remaining 2 tbsp of oil, ¼ tsp of chile flakes, 2 tsp of fennel seeds, the garlic, and the orange peel. Fry for 1 minute, until the garlic starts to lightly brown, then add the tomatoes and their juice, stock, water, ¾ tsp salt, and plenty of pepper. Cook for 2–3 minutes, or until boiling, then stir in the fried orzo. Cover, then decrease the heat to medium-low and simmer for 15 minutes, stirring once or twice throughout so the orzo cooks evenly. Remove the lid and cook for 1–2 minutes, until the consistency is like risotto. Stir in the shrimp and cook for 2–3 minutes, until they are pink. Stir in the basil and serve at once, with the marinated feta sprinkled on top.

Serves four

7 oz/200g feta, broken into ½–¾ inch/ 1–2cm pieces

½ tsp crushed red pepper flakes

4 tsp fennel seeds, toasted and lightly crushed

5 tbsp/75ml olive oil

1⅓ cups/250g orzo

salt and black pepper

3 garlic cloves, minced

1 orange, peel finely shaved to get 3 strips

1 (14.5 oz/400g) can chopped tomatoes

2 cups/500ml vegetable stock

¾ cup plus 2 tbsp/200ml water

14 oz/400g raw peeled shrimp

1½ cups/30g basil leaves, roughly shredded

Pasta with pecorino and pistachios

Serves four as a starter

2½ cups/50g basil leaves

1 garlic clove, crushed

3 anchovy fillets in oil, drained

5 tbsp/75ml olive oil

7 oz/200g dried trofie pasta (or fusilli)

2 cups/130g snow peas, thinly sliced on an angle

2½ oz/75g pecorino, finely shaved

½ cup plus 1 tbsp/ 75g shelled pistachios, roughly chopped

1 lemon: finely zest to get 1 tsp

salt and black pepper

Trofie is the traditional pasta to serve with pesto, but fusilli works just as well. For an extra twist of color and flavor, stir in some oven-dried tomatoes. Slice 14 oz/400g cherry tomatoes in half, toss with 1 tbsp olive oil and some salt and pepper, and roast at 350°F for 40 minutes, until semi-dried and slightly caramelized. A batch of these tomatoes will keep well for up to 1 week in a sealed container in the fridge, ready to be thrown in with all sorts of other salads and grains.

1. Place 1½ cups/30g of the basil in the bowl of a food processor with the garlic, anchovies, and olive oil. Blitz to form a rough paste and set aside.

2. Fill a large saucepan halfway with salted water and place over high heat. Once boiling, add the pasta and cook for about 7 minutes, until nearly al dente. Add the snow peas and cook together for another 2 minutes, until the pasta is just cooked and the snow peas are soft.

3. Reserving 2 tbsp of water, drain the pasta and snow peas and place in a large bowl. Add the basil paste and stir well. Add the pecorino, pistachios, lemon zest, the remaining 1 cup/20g of basil, ⅛ tsp salt, and a generous grind of pepper. Toss gently to combine and serve.

Anchovy and samphire spaghetti

Both samphire (a sea vegetable—you can substitute thin spears of asparagus) and anchovy pack a really salty punch. Combining the two results in a simple little dish that delivers big on flavor. Thanks to Claudia Lazarus.

1. Put the oil into a large sauté pan and place over medium heat. Once hot, add the anchovies, chile flakes, garlic, lemon zest, ½ cup of the parsley, and a good grind of pepper. Fry gently for 5 minutes, stirring frequently, until the anchovies have melted into the oil. Pour in the wine and cook for 4–5 minutes, until the sauce has thickened and reduced, then remove from the heat and set aside while you cook the pasta.

2. Bring a large pot of salted water to a boil and cook the spaghetti until al dente. Thirty seconds before the spaghetti is ready, add the samphire (to the same pot the pasta is cooking in). Reserve a couple of ladles of the pasta water, then drain the pasta and samphire. Return the sauté pan of sauce to medium-high heat. Add the cooked spaghetti and samphire and toss to combine. If you need to loosen the sauce, add a little of the reserved pasta water. Stir in the remaining ½ cup of parsley and another good grind of pepper, then divide among 4 plates.

3. Finish with a sprinkling of chile flakes and serve, with a lemon wedge on the side.

Serves four

5 tbsp/75ml olive oil

about 9 anchovy fillets in oil, drained and finely chopped (1½ tbsp)

1½ tsp Aleppo chile flakes, plus extra to serve (or ¾ tsp other crushed red pepper flakes)

1 garlic clove, minced

1 lemon: finely zest to get 1 tsp, then cut into 4 wedges, to serve

1 cup/20g parsley, finely chopped

black pepper

7 tbsp/100ml dry white wine

9 oz/250g spaghetti

9 oz/250g samphire or thin asparagus spears, cut into lengths

Gnocchi alla Romana

*Serves eight as a starter
(or eight kids)*

**6 tbsp/80g unsalted
 butter**

1 qt/1L whole milk

salt and black pepper

1½ cups/250g semolina
 (either fine or coarse)

**1 tsp finely grated
 nutmeg**

3½ oz/100g Parmesan,
 finely grated

2 egg yolks

**1½ oz/40g aged
 Cheddar,** finely grated

Comfort food does not get any more comforting than this. Serve this as it is, or with a crisp green salad. It's the ultimate family dish. I've yet to meet a kid who doesn't love it or an adult who doesn't think it's perfect with a glass of red wine. Make this up to the point it goes in the oven if you like and keep in the fridge for 1 day before baking.

1. Put the butter and milk into a medium saucepan with 1 tsp of salt and a good grind of black pepper. Place over medium-high heat. Once the butter has melted and the milk is simmering, remove from the heat and whisk in the semolina, nutmeg, Parmesan, and egg yolks until smooth and combined. Return to the heat and whisk continuously until thickened. Continue to cook and stir for 3–4 minutes, until the mixture comes away from the sides of the pan. Set aside to cool for 15 minutes; don't leave it for longer, or else it'll set too much and break when rolled.

2. Lay two large pieces of plastic wrap—about 12 x 16 inches/ 30 x 40cm—on your work surface and spoon half the mixture onto each piece. Roll to form 2 sausages—each about 1½ inches/ 4cm wide and 15 inches/38cm long—and keep in the fridge for at least 2 hours, until set. Preheat the oven to 400°F. Remove and discard the plastic, and then cut each sausage into ½-inch/1½cm rounds. Arrange the rounds in a shallow baking sheet, about 9 x 13 inches/23 x 33cm, in rows that slightly overlap. Sprinkle with Cheddar and bake for 15 minutes, until the cheese has melted.

3. Turn the oven to its highest broil setting and place the gnocchi about 4 inches/10cm beneath the heat. Broil for 2–3 minutes, until the top is golden brown. Let cool for 5 minutes before serving.

Meat

Lamb and feta meatballs

Serves six

1 lb 2 oz/500g ground lamb

3½ oz/100g feta, crumbled into ½-inch/1cm pieces

2 tbsp thyme leaves

2 garlic cloves, minced

½ cup/10g parsley, finely chopped

1 cup/45g fresh white breadcrumbs (from about 2 slices, crusts removed)

½ tsp ground cinnamon

salt and black pepper

1 tbsp olive oil

2 tsp pomegranate molasses (optional)

These work either as a main course, in a pita or with some rice and vegetables, or eaten as they are as a canapé before supper. If you do the latter, you'll make double the number of balls and they'll need less cooking—3–4 minutes in the pan, then 3 minutes in the oven to warm through. Once they've come out of the pan, put them on individual cocktail sticks (the wood skewers will be fine in the oven for such a short time, and then they'll be ready to serve). The pomegranate molasses is a delicious addition, with its distinct sweet-sharpness, but don't worry if you don't have it; the meatballs are still great without it. These can be fried up to 6 hours in advance and warmed through for 5 minutes before serving. Leftovers can also be eaten the next day, either at room temperature or warmed through.

1. Preheat the oven to 425°F.

2. Put the lamb into a large bowl with the feta, thyme, garlic, parsley, breadcrumbs, cinnamon, ¾ tsp salt, and plenty of pepper. Mix well to combine, then form into about 18 balls (or 36, if making them as a canapé): they should all be about 1½ inches/ 4cm in diameter and weigh about 1¼ oz/35g.

3. Put the oil into a large frying pan and place over medium-high heat. Once hot, add the meatballs and fry for 5–6 minutes, turning them over carefully throughout until golden brown on all sides. Transfer them to a parchment-lined baking pan, drizzle with the pomegranate molasses and bake for 5 minutes, until the meatballs are cooked through. Serve hot.

     Pictured on page 202

Beef sirloin and basil salad

This works either as an impressive starter or as a lunch or light supper. All the elements can be prepared a day in advance and kept in the fridge, but don't put the dish together until you're just about to serve because the leaves will wilt and the croutons don't like to sit around and mingle for too long.

1. Place 1¼ cups of the basil in the bowl of a food processor with the garlic, 5 tbsp/75ml of the oil, and a rounded ¼ tsp salt. Blitz to form a thick dressing and set aside.

2. Season the beef well with ¼ tsp salt and a generous grind of black pepper. Pour 1 tbsp of the oil into a medium frying pan and place over high heat. When the pan is very hot, add the beef and sear for 3–4 minutes (for medium-rare), turning after 1½–2 minutes. Remove from the pan and set aside to rest for 10 minutes.

3. Add the remaining 3 tbsp of oil to the same pan and place over high heat. When hot, add the pita bread and fry for 2–3 minutes, shaking the pan from time to time, until golden and crisp all over. Transfer to a paper towel–lined plate, sprinkle with a pinch of salt, and set aside.

4. Place the radicchio, arugula, lemon juice, Parmesan, basil oil, and the remaining ¼ cup of the basil leaves in a large serving bowl and set aside.

5. When ready to serve, slice the beef against the grain into ¼-inch/½cm slices. Sprinkle with a pinch of salt and add to the salad bowl. Add the pita pieces, toss gently, and serve at once.

Serves four

2½ cups/50g basil leaves

1 garlic clove, crushed

9 tbsp/135ml olive oil

salt

14 oz/400g top sirloin
   (2 steaks, each about
   ½ inch/1½cm thick)

black pepper

2 pita breads, roughly
   torn into 1¼-inch/
   3cm pieces (3 cups/120g)

**2 baby, oblong-shape
   red radicchio,** leaves
   separated, then sliced
   in half lengthwise
   (5¾ oz/160g)

2 cups/40g arugula

3 tbsp lemon juice

2¼ oz/60g Parmesan,
   shaved

Pictured on page 203

Lamb siniyah

This is the Middle Eastern equivalent of shepherd's pie, with a tahini crust standing in for the layer of mashed potato. It's a rich and comforting dish, making a star of both the tahini and the stewed lamb.

The stew can be made well in advance—a day or two ahead, if kept in the fridge or frozen—ready for the tahini sauce and baking. Serve with bulgur or rice.

Serves four to six

¼ **cup/60ml olive oil**

2 **small onions,** finely chopped (1¾ cups/250g)

6 **medium celery stalks,** thinly sliced (2 cups/250g)

1 **tsp tomato paste**

1 **tbsp baharat spice mix**

2 **lb 2 oz/1kg stewing lamb** (shoulder, leg, or neck), cut into ¾-inch/2cm chunks

salt and black pepper

1 **lb 2 oz/500g plum tomatoes,** roughly chopped

1 **tsp paprika**

½ **cup/60g pine nuts,** toasted

2 **cups/40g parsley,** chopped

TAHINI SAUCE

⅔ **cup/200g tahini**

1½ **tbsp lemon juice**

1 **garlic clove,** minced

⅔ **cup/160ml water**

salt

1. Put 2 tbsp of the oil into a 8-inch/20cm casserole pan and place over medium heat. Add the onions and celery and cook for 10–12 minutes, stirring from time to time, until soft. Add the tomato paste and baharat, cook for another 2 minutes, then tip into a large bowl. Keep the pan as it is; you don't need to rinse or wipe it.

2. Season the lamb with ¾ tsp salt and a good grind of black pepper. Add 1½ tsp of the oil to the same pan and place over medium-high heat. Add a quarter of the lamb and fry for 3 minutes, turning throughout so that all sides get browned. Transfer to the bowl of onions and repeat with the remaining lamb, adding 1½ tsp of the oil to the pan with each batch. Return all the lamb and vegetables to the pan and stir in two-thirds of the tomatoes, the paprika, ½ tsp salt, and plenty of black pepper. Bring to a boil, then turn the heat to medium-low and simmer gently for about 70 minutes, covered, until the meat is very tender and the sauce is thick. You might need to remove the lid for the last 5 or 10 minutes, for the sauce to thicken up. Stir in the pine nuts, parsley, and remaining tomatoes and set aside.

3. About 10 minutes before the meat is ready, preheat the oven to 400°F.

4. To make the tahini sauce, whisk the tahini, lemon juice, garlic, the water, and ¼ tsp salt in a medium bowl. The consistency should be pourable—thick like heavy cream—so add a bit more water if you need to. Pour this evenly over the lamb and bake, covered, for 20 minutes, until the tahini sauce has thickened. Uncover the pan and bake for another 20 minutes, uncovered, for the tahini crust to turn golden brown.

5. Remove from the oven, let rest for 5 minutes, and then serve.

Grilled lamb fillet with almonds and orange blossom

Serves six

6 garlic cloves, minced

5 lemons: finely zest 2 to get 1 tbsp, then juice all to get ½ cup plus 2 tbsp/150ml

3 tbsp thyme leaves

¾ cup/180ml olive oil

salt and black pepper

2 lb 2 oz/1kg lamb neck fillets (about 8 fillets)

1 cup plus 3 tbsp/170g almonds

1 tbsp honey

½ tsp orange blossom water

3 red bell peppers, cut into quarters and seeded (13 oz/370g)

1 cup/20g mint leaves, finely chopped

This is a great dish for feeding friends, as you can get much of the work done in advance. The day before, the meat can be seared, the bell peppers can be grilled, and the sauce can be made, but hold back on the mint, as it will discolor. Keep everything in the fridge and when ready to serve, just finish off the meat in the oven and add the mint to the sauce.

If you're searing the meat in advance and keeping it in the fridge until cooking, make sure you take it out of the fridge a good hour before you cook it; it needs to be room temperature rather than fridge-cold. Also note the longer amount of time it will need in the oven to warm through—15 minutes rather than 3 or 4.

I cook this on the barbecue during the summer, but instructions here are for a stove top. I also tend to make more nuts than I need and sprinkle them over all sorts of other things—roasted cauliflower or a plate of roasted peppers work particularly well.

1. Put the garlic into a large bowl with 2 tsp of the lemon zest, 6 tbsp/90ml of the lemon juice, the thyme, 6 tbsp/90ml of the oil, 1½ tsp salt, and a really good grind of pepper. Add the lamb, mix very well, then leave in the fridge for at least 2 hours (or overnight) to marinate.

2. Heat 2 tbsp of the oil in a small pan or frying pan and add the almonds. Cook for 3–4 minutes, stirring continuously, until the nuts are golden brown and evenly cooked. Remove from the heat and set aside to cool a little. Using a slotted spoon, remove the nuts. Roughly chop the nuts and put them into a bowl. Discard the cooking oil. Add the remaining 1 tsp of lemon zest to the nuts along with the remaining ¼ cup/60ml of lemon juice, the honey, orange blossom water, ½ tsp salt, a good grind of black pepper, and 3 tbsp of the oil. Mix well and set aside until ready to serve.

3. Preheat the oven to 450°F.

4. Place a large ridged griddle pan over high heat and ventilate your kitchen well. Drizzle the peppers with the remaining 1 tablespoon of olive oil and ¼ tsp salt and place on the griddle. Cook for about 10 minutes, turning once after 5 minutes, until charred on both sides.

5. Put the lamb pieces on the piping hot griddle (reserve the marinade) and cook for about 4 minutes, turning after 2 minutes, until both sides are charred and starting to caramelize. If you are serving straightaway, transfer the lamb to a roasting pan, along with the peppers, and roast for 3–4 minutes for medium-rare (145°F on a meat thermometer) or a few minutes longer if you like it well cooked. If you are cooking the lamb from room temperature (having kept it in the fridge after searing), it will need 15 minutes in the oven at this stage. Either way, timings will depend on the thickness of the meat. Once the lamb is cooked, remove it from the oven, cover the pan with foil and let the lamb rest for 5–10 minutes.

6. Meanwhile, place the marinade in a small saucepan and bring to a boil over medium–high heat. Remove from the heat and set aside.

7. When you are ready to serve, carve the lamb into ½-inch/1cm slices and arrange on a platter with the red peppers. Spoon on the marinade, add the mint to the almond sauce, and spoon some on top. Serve any remaining sauce on the side.

Lamb meatloaf with tahini sauce and tomatoes

This can be served two ways. Either as it is, warm, as part of a main meal, or left to cool and set, then cut into thick slices. This will keep in the fridge for up to 2 days. These slices are great piled into a sandwich or warm pita bread, with the tahini sauce and grated tomato drizzled on top. Either way, it's a super family-friendly recipe.

Makes one loaf, to serve six to eight

1 zucchini, roughly chopped (1 ½ cups/160g)	**3 oz/80g pecorino,** finely grated
1 carrot, roughly chopped (⅔ cup/100g)	**1 cup/50g fresh white breadcrumbs** (from about 2 slices, crusts left on if soft)
1 large onion, roughly chopped (1 cup/180g)	
3 small tomatoes: 1 roughly chopped, 2 coarsely grated and skin discarded (¾ cup/180g)	**2 large eggs**
	2 tbsp tomato paste
	2 tsp ground cumin
	2 tsp ground allspice
	salt
1 lb 2 oz/500g ground lamb	**⅓ cup/100g tahini**
	1 tbsp lemon juice
4 garlic cloves, minced	**5 tbsp/70 ml water**

1. Preheat the oven to 400°F and grease a 8 x 4-inch/20 x 10cm loaf pan with a little oil.

2. Place the zucchini, carrot, onion, and chopped tomato in the bowl of a food processor and blitz to combine; you want the consistency to be similar to that of the ground lamb. Transfer the vegetables

to a sieve set over a bowl and squeeze them to get rid of as much liquid as possible. Put the vegetables into a large bowl with the ground lamb, 2 of the garlic cloves, the pecorino, breadcrumbs, eggs, tomato paste, cumin, allspice, and 1 tsp salt. Bring the mixture together until well combined, then transfer to the loaf pan.

3. Place the loaf pan inside a high-sided baking dish. Carefully fill the baking dish with enough boiling water to rise halfway up the sides of the loaf pan. Transfer to the oven and bake for 1 hour and 10 minutes, until golden brown.

4. While the meatloaf is cooking, prepare the tahini sauce. Put the tahini, the remaining 2 garlic cloves, lemon juice, and ¼ tsp salt into a medium bowl. Slowly whisk in the water until you get a smooth, thick sauce. Set aside until ready to serve.

5. Once the meatloaf has cooked, remove the pan from the water bath and leave to cool for 10 minutes. Drain away and discard the liquid and fat from the loaf pan, then, using a wide spatula, transfer the meatloaf to a platter. Pour one-third of the tahini sauce over the meatloaf, followed by one-third of the grated tomato.

6. Serve warm, with the remaining tahini and tomato alongside, or leave to cool and cut into slices to serve in sandwiches.

Lamb arayes with tahini and sumac

Makes eight, to serve four

FILLING

1 lb 2 oz/500g ground lamb

½ **small onion,** coarsely grated (½ cup/60g)

1½ **small tomatoes,** coarsely grated and skin discarded (½ cup/140g)

1 tsp ground allspice

⅓ **cup/90g tahini**

2 garlic cloves, minced

2 tsp pomegranate molasses

1 cup/20g mint, finely shredded

salt

8 (8-inch/20cm) flour or corn tortillas

3 oz/80g aged Cheddar, coarsely grated

¼ **cup/60ml olive oil,** plus 2 tsp for brushing

1 tbsp sumac

Arayes are lamb stuffed flatbreads popular across the Middle East. They're traditionally made with pita bread but I've used tortillas here. They're great for lunch or as a snack before supper, served with a fresh chopped salad or some sumac yogurt sauce (page 217). They're quick and easy to make, but if you want to make things even quicker and easier, the filling can be made up to 1 day ahead and kept in the fridge. You're then all set to just fill and fry. Thanks to Sami Tamimi, for bringing these (along with so many other tasty things) to the ongoing feast.

1. Mix together all the ingredients for the filling in a large bowl with 1 tsp salt. Taking one tortilla at a time, spoon about 1 cup/100g of filling over half the tortilla, leaving a border of ¼ inch/½cm around the edges. Sprinkle the meat lightly with cheese and then fold the tortilla over, to make a semi-circle. Press down gently so that the meat is evenly spread and ½ inch/1cm thick. Continue with the remaining tortillas, meat, and cheese in the same way.

2. Put 1 tbsp oil into a large nonstick frying pan and place over medium-low heat. Once hot, add 2 of the folded tortillas and fry gently for 2–3 minutes. Turn over and cook for another 2–3 minutes, until the tortilla is golden brown on both sides and the meat is cooked through. Transfer to a plate, sprinkle with a pinch of salt, and set aside. Using a paper towel, wipe the pan clean of all the lamb juices and continue in the same way with the remaining oil and tortillas.

3. Mix the remaining 2 tsp oil with the sumac. Brush lightly over the tops of the arayes, and serve warm or at room temperature.

Slow-cooked lamb shoulder with mint and cumin

This is a feast of a meal when served with something like lima beans—gently mashed with the cooking juices from the lamb—and a simple green salad. Get the lamb marinating overnight in the fridge, if you can, for the flavors to really seep into the meat. If you're planning to eat it on the day you're cooking, 4 or 5 hours is long enough, but you'll have to get going first thing because it also needs 6½ hours in the oven. If you want to really get ahead, the lamb can also be cooked 1 day in advance and kept in the fridge, ready to be shredded and warmed up in its own juices.

1. Place the lemon zest, lemon juice, garlic, spices, herbs, and oil in the bowl of a food processor with 1½ tsp salt and plenty of pepper. Blitz to form a rough paste and set aside.

2. Place the lamb in a large bowl and poke the meat all over about 30 times with a small sharp knife. Rub the spice paste all over the meat, massaging it into the incisions. Cover with plastic wrap and refrigerate for at least 4 hours (or overnight, ideally) for the flavors to develop.

3. Preheat the oven to 375°F.

4. Transfer the lamb, along with all the marinade, into a large high-sided baking dish, about 12 x 16 inches/30 x 40cm. Cover the dish tightly with foil and roast for 1 hour. Reduce the temperature to 350°F and add the celery root, carrots, and garlic (cut side up) to the dish. Continue to roast for 4 hours, basting the meat and vegetables three or four times during cooking (and resealing the tray with the foil each time). Remove the foil and return to the oven for a final 1½ hours, until the lamb is browned all over, the meat is falling apart, and the vegetables are caramelized.

Serves four to six

2 lemons: finely zest to get 1 tbsp, then juice to get ¼ cup

6 garlic cloves, crushed

1 tbsp paprika

½ tsp fenugreek seeds, lightly crushed

2 tsp ground cumin

1¼ cups/25g mint leaves

¾ cup/15g cilantro

3 tbsp olive oil

salt and black pepper

1 large lamb shoulder (4½ lb/2kg)

½ celery root, peeled and cut into 1¼-inch/3cm wedges (8 cups/850g)

5 large carrots, peeled and chopped in half crosswise (1 lb 5 oz/600g)

2 heads of garlic, sliced in half crosswise

Lamb and pistachio patties with sumac yogurt sauce

These patties are lovely as a snack or as part of a feast at a barbecue. If you want to make them into a more substantial meal, however, just serve them with some arugula tossed with olive oil, lemon juice, and shaved Parmesan. The yogurt sauce can be made the day before. The patties will keep in the fridge for 1 day uncooked, or they can be cooked up to 6 hours in advance, ready to be warmed through for 5 minutes before serving. Leftovers are also good the next day, at room temperature or warmed through.

1. Mix together all the ingredients for the sumac yogurt sauce and keep in the fridge until needed.

2. To make the patties, put the pistachios into the bowl of a food processor. Blitz for a few seconds, to roughly chop, then put into a medium bowl. Add the arugula to the processor, blitz for a few seconds to roughly chop, then add to the bowl of pistachios. Continue with the onion and garlic, to form a smooth paste, and add to the bowl. Add the lamb, 1 tbsp of oil, ¾ tsp salt, and a good grind of pepper. Mix well to combine, then, with wet hands, shape the mix into about twenty patties. They should each be about 2 inches/5cm wide, ¾ inch/2cm thick, and weigh about 1½ oz/40g.

3. Put 1 tbsp of the oil into a large nonstick frying pan and place over medium heat. Once hot, add the patties—as many as you can fit without crowding the pan—and cook for 7 minutes, turning after 3½ minutes, until golden brown and just cooked through. Keep warm while you repeat with the remaining patties. If you need to, add another tbsp oil to the pan during the process. When the patties are all cooked, pile them onto a large platter and serve with the sumac yogurt sauce.

Makes about twenty patties, to serve four as a main or six as a snack

SUMAC YOGURT SAUCE

1 cup/250g Greek-style yogurt

1 tbsp sumac

1 tbsp olive oil

1 tbsp lemon juice

½ cup/60g shelled pistachios

1¼ cups/25g arugula

1 onion, quartered (5¼ oz/150g)

1 large garlic clove, peeled

1 lb 2 oz/500g ground lamb

about 3 tbsp olive oil

salt and black pepper

Spiced "shepherd's pie"
with lima bean crust

Serves six

6 tbsp/90ml olive oil

3 garlic cloves, minced

3 shallots, thinly sliced

1 lb 5 oz/600g ground lamb

2 tsp cumin seeds

1 tbsp ground allspice

2 lemons, finely zested

salt

3 tbsp tomato paste

3 tbsp rose harissa (or
   50 percent more or less,
   depending on variety;
   see page 301)

**3½ oz/100g dried
   apricots,** quartered

**1 cup plus 3 tbsp/280ml
   chicken stock**

**¾ cup plus 3 tbsp/
   220ml white wine**

**⅔ cup/80g pitted green
   olives,** halved

**4 cups/670g cooked lima
   beans** (three 15.5 oz/
   440g cans, drained, or
   2½ cups/400g uncooked
   beans, soaked overnight
   and cooked)

¼ cup/70g tahini

3 tbsp water

black pepper

If Lamb siniyah (see page 206) is a Middle Eastern take on the shepherd's pie, then this is my North African take, with a lima bean mash standing in for the potatoes. It's rich, comforting, and hearty, needing little more than a green salad or roasted carrots alongside. Make this up to 2 days in advance, to the point where it goes in the oven. If baked straight from the fridge it will need an extra 5–10 minutes. Without the mash, it can be frozen for 1 month.

1. Put 3 tbsp of oil into a large heavy-bottom pan with a lid and place over medium-high heat. Add the garlic and shallots and sauté for 5 minutes, stirring frequently, until soft and golden. Increase the heat to high and add the lamb, cumin, allspice, half the lemon zest, and ½ tsp salt. Fry for 5 minutes, until browned, stirring every now and then, then add the tomato paste, harissa, and apricots. Fry for another 2 minutes, then pour in the stock and wine. Decrease the heat to medium and simmer, covered, for 30 minutes. Once cooked, set aside to cool, then add the olives. Spoon into a 8 x 10-inch/20 x 25cm ovenproof high-sided dish and refrigerate for at least 30 minutes. This will firm up the meat, making it easier to spread the mash on top.

2. Preheat the oven to 400°F.

3. To make the mash, mix the lima beans in a bowl with the remaining lemon zest, 2 tbsp of the olive oil, the tahini, water, ¾ tsp salt, and a grind of black pepper. Use a potato masher to mash the beans; they don't need to be completely smooth, just spreadable. Spread the mash over the lamb, then use a spoon to make a few shallow divots. Drizzle with the remaining 1 tbsp of oil and bake for 30 minutes, until nicely colored and bubbly. Rest for 10 minutes before serving.

Arnold's roast chicken with caraway and cranberry stuffing

Arnold Rogow was a family friend of Ixta Belfrage, who tested a lot of the Ottolenghi SIMPLE *recipes with Esme. Ixta has a habit of giving all the credit to others, including the inspiration behind this dish, but I've no doubt Arnold would have been calling this Ixta's roast chicken. Make the stuffing and prep the chicken up to 1 day ahead, then just keep in the fridge and bring to room temperature before roasting.*

1. To make the marinade, melt 2 tbsp/30g of butter and stir in 3 tsp of the caraway seeds, 2 of the garlic cloves, the sugar, and ½ tsp salt. Place the chicken in a large bowl, rub the marinade all over it, and set aside.

2. Preheat the oven to 400°F.

3. To make the stuffing, put the remaining 3 tbsp/40g butter into a large nonstick pan and place over medium-high heat. Add the remaining 2 tsp of caraway seeds and fry for 2 minutes, until fragrant. Add the remaining 5 garlic cloves, the celery, onion, cranberries, chestnuts, and 1 tsp salt. Fry for 12–13 minutes, stirring often, until golden and softened. Tip into a medium bowl and stir in the bread, parsley, and stock.

4. Transfer the chicken to a small roasting pan. Sprinkle with a generous pinch of salt and a grind of pepper and fill the cavity with the stuffing. Place any leftover stuffing in an ovenproof dish and put it into the oven 30–35 minutes after the chicken goes into the oven.

5. Roast the chicken for 70–75 minutes, basting every 20 minutes, until the skin is golden brown and crisp and the juices run clear when a knife is inserted into the thickest part of the thigh. Remove from the oven and set aside to rest for 10 minutes before serving.

Serves 4

5 tbsp/70g unsalted butter

5 tsp caraway seeds, toasted and lightly crushed

7 garlic cloves, minced

1 tbsp dark brown sugar

salt

1 whole chicken (about 3 lb/1.4kg)

5–6 large celery stalks, cut into ½-inch/1cm dice (3 cups/300g)

1 onion, cut into ½-inch/1cm dice (scant 1 cup/140g)

3½ oz/100g dried cranberries

3½ oz/100g ready-cooked and peeled chestnuts, roughly chopped

4–5 slices mixed rye and wheat sourdough bread, crusts removed, lightly toasted, then roughly torn into ¾-inch/2cm pieces (3⅓ cups/100g)

¾ cup/15g parsley, roughly chopped

½ cup/120ml chicken stock

black pepper

Beef meatballs with lemon and celery root

Serves four

14 oz/400g ground beef

1 medium onion, finely chopped (scant 1 cup/140g)

3 cups/120g fresh white breadcrumbs (from about 4 slices, crusts removed)

1 cup/20g parsley, chopped, plus extra to garnish

1 large egg, beaten

¾ tsp ground allspice

salt and black pepper

2 tbsp olive oil

1 medium celery root, peeled, quartered, then each quarter cut crosswise into ½-inch/1cm slices (4 cups/400g)

3 garlic cloves, minced

½ tsp ground turmeric

1½ tsp fennel seeds, lightly crushed

1 tsp sweet smoked paprika

2 cups/500ml chicken stock

3½ tbsp lemon juice

I often say that my favorite food is the sort that can, at once, comfort, surprise, and delight. This dish (as is often the case with meatballs) does all these things for me. The meatballs have all the comfort of a home-cooked meal, with the lemon and celery root providing the surprise and delight. These are lovely as they are, served with some couscous or rice to soak up the juices, or with a little bit of Greek-style yogurt on the side. The dish can be made a day in advance and kept in the fridge. Reheat before serving.

1. Put the beef, onion, breadcrumbs, parsley, egg, allspice, ½ tsp salt, and some black pepper into a large bowl. Using your hands, mix well, then form into about 20 balls. Each ball should weigh about 1½ oz/40g.

2. Put the oil into a large sauté pan with a lid and place over high heat. Add the meatballs and sear for about 5 minutes, turning so that all sides are golden brown. Transfer the meatballs to a separate plate and add the celery root, garlic, turmeric, fennel, and paprika to the pan. Cook over high heat, stirring, for 2 minutes, until the garlic has taken on a bit of color and the spices smell aromatic. Return the meatballs to the pan and add the stock, lemon juice, ½ tsp salt, and some black pepper. Bring to a boil, then simmer gently over medium-low heat, covered, for 30 minutes. Remove the lid and leave to bubble away for about 10 minutes, for the sauce to thicken up.

3. Remove the pan from the heat and allow it to sit for 5 or 10 minutes. Serve, along with a final sprinkle of parsley.

Pictured on page 222

Ricotta and oregano meatballs

Using ricotta makes the meatballs super light and fluffy. The dish can be made a day in advance, kept in the fridge, and then reheated.

1. First make the tomato sauce. Put 2 tbsp of the oil into a sauté pan and place over medium-high heat. Add half the onions, half the garlic, and half the oregano and cook for 8–10 minutes, stirring until the onions have softened without taking on color. Add the tomatoes and their juice, half the stock, ½ tsp salt, and some black pepper. Decrease the temperature to medium and cook for 10–15 minutes, stirring from time to time, to thicken the sauce.

2. Meanwhile, make the meatballs. Place the remaining onion, garlic, and oregano in a large bowl along with the beef, breadcrumbs, ricotta, Parmesan, egg, parsley, ¾ tsp salt, and some black pepper. Using your hands, mix everything together and shape into 12–14 balls.

3. Put 1 tbsp of the oil into a large frying pan and, when hot, add the meatballs (you will need to do this in two batches, adding another tbsp of oil to the pan for the next batch). Sear for 8 minutes, turning throughout, then transfer to a separate plate.

4. Gently lower the meatballs into the sauce and pour over enough of the remaining stock so that the meatballs are almost covered. Add a little water, if needed, to make up the liquid. Place over medium-low heat and simmer very gently, covered, for 30 minutes. To thicken the sauce—it should have the consistency of a thick pasta sauce—remove the lid toward the end of cooking and increase the temperature a little. Remove from the heat and set aside for at least 10 minutes. Add extra oregano and serve.

Serves four

¼ cup/60ml olive oil

2 large onions, chopped (2⅓ cups/330g)

4 garlic cloves, minced

1 cup/20g oregano leaves, chopped, plus extra to serve

1 (14.5 oz/400g) can chopped tomatoes

2 cups/500ml chicken stock

salt and black pepper

1 lb 2 oz/500g ground beef

2 cups/100g fresh white breadcrumbs (from 3–4 slices, crusts removed)

9 oz/250g ricotta

2¼ oz/60g Parmesan, grated

1 large egg, beaten

1 cup/20g parsley, chopped

Pictured on page 223

Harissa beef sirloin with pepper and lemon sauce

This is a great dish to feed friends if you like knowing that all the work that needs doing is done well before anyone arrives. The pepper sauce can be made 1 day ahead. You can also marinate the meat for 1 day and it can be seared in advance too. Keep separate in the fridge, bring everything back to room temperature before serving or cooking, and the meal can be on the table 15 minutes after the stove is turned on. This works well with the Oven fries with oregano and feta (page 138) and a crisp green salad.

Serves four

2 large top sirloin steaks, trimmed (1 lb 5 oz/600g)

1½ tbsp rose harissa (or 50 percent more or less, depending on variety; see page 301)

flaked sea salt and black pepper

2 large red or yellow bell peppers (14 oz/400g)

2 tbsp olive oil

1 garlic clove, minced

1 (14.5 oz/400g) can of chopped tomatoes

½ tsp crushed red pepper flakes

¼ tsp paprika

½ small preserved lemon, seeds discarded, skin and flesh roughly chopped (2 tbsp)

½ cup/10g parsley, roughly chopped, plus extra to serve

1 lemon, quartered, for serving

1. Place the beef in a bowl and add the harissa, ½ tsp salt, and some black pepper. Brush or rub the harissa into the meat, then leave to marinate for at least 1 hour (or in the fridge if you are marinating

overnight). If leaving in the fridge, be sure to bring the meat back to room temperature before cooking.

2. To make the sauce, preheat the broiler and cook the peppers for 20–25 minutes, turning twice, until charred all over. Place in a bowl, cover with plastic wrap, then, once cool enough to handle, remove the pepper skins and cut the flesh into long, thin strips. Discard the skin and seeds.

3. Put the oil into a medium frying pan and place over medium heat. Add the garlic, cook for 1 minute or so, then add the tomatoes and their juice, pepper flakes, paprika, $\frac{1}{2}$ tsp salt, and some black pepper. Bring to a gentle simmer, cook for 7 minutes, then add the bell pepper, preserved lemon, and parsley. Cook for another 7 minutes, or until the sauce thickens but is still easy to pour. Set aside to come to room temperature.

4. Place a frying pan over high heat. Once smoking hot, add the steaks and cook for 4–5 minutes, turning after 2 minutes, until caramelized on both sides. Remove from the pan, sprinkle with a good pinch of salt, and rest for 10 minutes.

5. Serve the meat warm or at room temperature, sliced into $\frac{1}{2}$-inch/1cm strips, with the sauce spooned on top or alongside. Sprinkle with parsley and serve with a wedge of lemon alongside.

Spring roast chicken with preserved lemon

I'm not the first to combine lemon, garlic, and chicken—and I won't be the last—but sometimes it's good to be reminded that the classics are classics for a reason. Roasting a chicken is the ultimate simple dish. It's easy, quick, fills the house with delicious smells, and everyone loves the result. You can prep the chicken 4–5 hours in advance if you like, and then just place in the oven when ready to cook.

1. Preheat the oven to 400°F.

2. Place the butter, thyme, garlic, preserved lemon, lemon zest, ¼ tsp salt, and a generous grind of pepper in a food processor. Blitz to combine.

3. With the chicken's legs pointing toward you, use your hands to loosen the skin away from the breasts and spread most of the butter mixture evenly under the skin and over the breasts. Spread the remaining butter over the legs.

4. Place the chicken in a medium high-sided baking pan, drizzle with the lemon juice, and sprinkle with ½ tsp salt and plenty of pepper. Roast for roughly 70 minutes, basting every 20 minutes or so, until the skin is golden brown and crisp and the juices run clear when the meat is pierced with a small knife.

5. Remove from the oven and set aside to rest for 10 minutes before serving.

Serves four

5 tbsp/70g unsalted butter, at room temperature

3 tbsp thyme leaves

3 garlic cloves, crushed

½ small preserved lemon, seeds discarded, flesh and skin roughly chopped (2½ tbsp)

1 lemon: finely zest to get 1 tsp, then juice to get 1½ tbsp

salt and black pepper

1 whole chicken (3⅓ lb/1.5kg)

Chicken Marbella

This is a dish I regularly cook for friends. All the work is done in advance—you can marinate it for up to 2 days in the fridge—and then it's just into the baking pan and into the oven when you're ready. The chicken loves the long marination but it can also be cooked straightaway, if you don't have the time. If you're going to do this, just season the chicken with the 1 tsp of salt and pepper (which would otherwise go into the marinade), rubbing it thoroughly into the skin before combining it with the rest of the marinade ingredients (no more salt required) and bake according to the recipe. I like to use chicken legs but others prefer chicken supremes (chicken breasts with the wing bone attached), which also work very well. Thanks to Julee Rosso and Sheila Lukins's The Silver Palate, *whose recipe for Chicken Marbella inspired this recipe.*

1. Place the chicken in a large nonreactive bowl and add the garlic, oregano, vinegar, oil, olives, capers, dates, and bay leaves, along with 1 tsp salt and a good grind of black pepper. Gently mix everything together, cover the bowl, and leave in the fridge to marinate for 1–2 days, stirring the ingredients a few times during the process.

2. Preheat the oven to 400°F.

3. Spread out the chicken legs on a medium high-sided baking pan, along with all the marinade ingredients. Whisk together the wine and molasses and pour over the meat. Place in the oven and cook for 50 minutes, basting two or three times, until the meat is golden brown on top and cooked through.

4. Remove from the oven, transfer everything to a large platter, sprinkle with some oregano, and serve.

Serves four generously

8 chicken legs (skin on and bone in) skin scored a few times (3 lb/1.4g)

5 garlic cloves, minced

¾ cup/15g fresh oregano leaves, plus extra to serve

3 tbsp red wine vinegar

3 tbsp olive oil

1 cup/100g pitted green olives

6 tbsp/60g capers, plus 2 tbsp of their brine

4¼ oz/120g Medjool dates, pitted and quartered lengthwise

2 bay leaves

salt and black pepper

½ cup/120ml dry white wine

1 tbsp date molasses (or standard molasses)

Chicken with miso, ginger, and lime

Serves six

8 chicken legs (skin
  on and bone in), skin
  scored a few times
  (3 lb/1.4kg)

2 tbsp sunflower oil

salt

2½ tbsp mirin

2½ tbsp maple syrup

2½ tbsp soy sauce

¼ cup/80g white miso

**2½-inch/6cm piece
  of fresh ginger,**
  peeled and finely
  grated (3 tbsp)

3 garlic cloves, minced

1 lime: peel shaved into
  fine strips, then juiced

**1½ oz/40g cilantro
  stems,** cut into
  2½-inch/6cm lengths

2 red chiles, sliced in
  half lengthwise

12 green onions:
  10 sliced in half
  lengthwise, 2 thinly
  sliced, to serve
  (4¼ oz/120g)

This dish is lovely either warm from the oven—served with sticky or basmati rice—or at room temperature. If you want to get ahead, and are cooking it the day before, keep it in the fridge overnight and take it out a half hour before serving; you don't want it fridge-cold.

1. Preheat the oven to 425°F.

2. Place the chicken legs in a large bowl with the oil and ¾ tsp salt. Mix together.

3. Place a large frying pan over medium-high heat. Once hot, add half the chicken legs, skin side down, and sear for 4–5 minutes, until golden brown. Turn over, cook for another 4–5 minutes, then remove from the pan. Repeat with the remaining chicken, discarding the fat as you go, and set aside.

4. Place the mirin, maple syrup, soy sauce, miso, ginger, garlic, lime strips, and lime juice in a large bowl. Whisk to combine, then add the chicken and stir well, so that everything is coated. Put the cilantro, chiles, and the 10 halved green onions into a high-sided baking dish (about 9 x 13 inches/24 x 36cm) and place the chicken on top, skin side up. Cover the dish tightly with foil and bake for 20 minutes. Remove the foil, turn the chicken legs over (skin side down), and return the dish to the oven for 30 minutes uncovered, turning the legs back over after 15 minutes (skin side up) and basting a couple of times. The chicken will be golden brown, sticky, and tender and the chiles and green onions will be soft.

5. To serve, place a chicken leg on each plate and surround it with the cilantro, chile, and halved green onions. Finally, drizzle with the sauce and sprinkle with the thinly sliced green onions.

     Pictured on page 232

Pork with ginger, green onion, and eggplant

This is one of my go-to easy suppers. Get all your chopping done for the things that go in with the pork before you turn on the stove. Once the heat is on, you'll want to be throwing things in the pan and stirring, rather than being under pressure to chop. You can make the pork up to 1 day in advance; keep in the fridge and warm through before serving. Serve as it is or with plain rice or noodles.

1. Place the eggplant in a large bowl with 1½ tsp salt. Mix well, then transfer to a basket steamer (or a colander that can sit over a large saucepan) and set aside.

2. Fill a large saucepan with enough water to rise 1¼ inches/3cm up the side. Bring to a boil over high heat, then place the steamer (or colander) in the pan. Cover with the lid or seal well with foil, to prevent the steam escaping. Decrease the temperature to medium-high and steam for 12 minutes. Remove and set aside.

3. Meanwhile, pour 2 tbsp of the peanut oil into a large sauté pan and place over high heat. Add the green onions, ginger, garlic, and chile and fry for 5 minutes, stirring often, until the garlic starts to color. Transfer to a bowl and set aside. Pour the remaining 2 tbsp of peanut oil into the pan and add the pork. Fry for 3 minutes, stirring to break up the meat. Add the mirin, soy sauce, keçap manis, sesame oil, rice vinegar, and ½ tsp salt. Cook for 2 minutes, then return the green onion mixture to the pan. Cook for 1 minute, then remove from the heat—there should be plenty of liquid— and stir in ½ cup/10g of the cilantro and the peanuts. Serve with the eggplant, sesame seeds, and remaining ¼ cup of cilantro.

Serves four

3 eggplant, cut into 1¼-inch/3cm dice (12 cups/950g)

salt

¼ cup/60ml peanut oil

2 or 3 bunches of green onions, chopped on an angle into 1¼-inch/ 3cm slices (3½ cups/250g)

2¾-inch/7cm piece of ginger, peeled and julienned (6 tbsp/60g)

4 garlic cloves, thinly sliced

1 green chile, thinly sliced

1 lb 2 oz/500g ground pork

3 tbsp mirin

2 tbsp dark soy sauce (avoid premium dark soy sauce, which is too dominant for the dish)

2 tbsp keçap manis or other sweet soy sauce

1 tsp sesame oil

1½ tbsp rice vinegar

¾ cup/15g cilantro, roughly chopped

½ cup/60g roasted and salted peanuts

1 tbsp sesame seeds, toasted

Pictured on page 233

Seeded chicken schnitzel

If you get hooked on this simple supper dish—and I believe the chances are pretty good—make an extra batch of the seed and breadcrumb mix. It keeps well in an airtight container for about 1 month and is really useful to have on hand. It works as well on strips of white fish or sticks of butternut squash as it does on the chicken.

1. Place the meat between two bits of plastic wrap, then, one at a time, gently flatten them with a rolling pin; they should end up about ½ inch/1cm thick.

2. In a medium bowl, mix the flour with ¼ tsp salt and some black pepper.

3. Put the eggs into a second bowl.

4. In a third bowl, mix the panko, both sesame seeds, sunflower seeds, coriander, turmeric, cayenne, and ¾ tsp salt.

5. Dip each bit of chicken into the flour and gently shake off the excess. Now dip it into the egg, then into the seed mix, to coat well. Repeat with the remaining chicken.

6. Put enough oil into a large frying pan to rise ¼ inch/½cm up the sides and place over medium heat. Once hot, add the chicken in batches and fry for 5–6 minutes, turning after 2½ minutes, until cooked through and golden brown on both sides. Transfer to a paper towel–lined plate while you continue with the remaining batch and serve hot, with the wedges of lemon alongside.

Serves four

4 boneless, skinless chicken breasts, each piece cut into 3 long strips (1 lb 5 oz/600g)

⅓ **cup/50g all-purpose flour**

salt and black pepper

2 eggs, lightly beaten

1⅓ **cups/80g panko crumbs**

6 tbsp/60g white sesame seeds

2 tbsp black sesame seeds (or extra white, if not available)

4½ **tbsp/40g sunflower seeds,** roughly chopped

1½ **tbsp coriander seeds,** roughly crushed

1 tsp ground turmeric

½ **tsp cayenne pepper**

about 7 tbsp/100ml sunflower oil, for frying

1 lemon, quartered, to serve

Slow-cooked chicken with a crisp corn crust

Serves six

3 tbsp olive oil

2 medium-large red onions, thinly sliced (5 cups/500g)

2 garlic cloves, minced

3 tbsp rose harissa (or 50 percent more or less, depending on variety; see page 301)

2 tsp sweet smoked paprika

1 lb 14 oz/850g boneless, skinless chicken thighs (9 or 10 thighs)

salt and black pepper

¾ cup plus 2 tbsp/200ml passata (tomato puree)

5 large tomatoes, quartered (14 oz/400g)

1½ cups/350ml water

1 cup/200g jarred roasted red peppers, drained and cut into ¾-inch/2cm thick rounds

½ oz/15g dark chocolate (70% cacao)

1 cup/20g cilantro, roughly chopped

This is a wonderful meal on an autumn day, served with a crisp green salad. The slow-cooked chicken is packed full of flavor and the crust—gluten-free, rich, and corny—makes for a welcome (and lighter) change to a heavier mash.

You can make the chicken well in advance if you want to get ahead. It keeps in the fridge for up to 3 days or can be frozen for 1 month. You want it to go into the oven defrosted, though, so it will need thawing before baking. The batter needs to be made fresh and spooned on top of the chicken just before the dish gets baked. It can also be baked a few hours in advance—just warm through for 10 minutes, covered in foil, before serving. I love the combination of the chicken and the corn, but the chicken also works well as it is, served on top of rice, in a wrap, or with a buttery baked potato.

1. Heat the oil in a large sauté pan with a lid over medium-high heat. Add the onions and fry for 8–9 minutes, stirring a few times, until caramelized and soft. Decrease the heat to medium and add the garlic, harissa, paprika, chicken, 1 tsp salt, and a good grind of black pepper. Cook for 5 minutes longer, stirring frequently, then add the tomato puree and tomatoes. Add the water, bring to a boil, then simmer over medium heat, covered, for 30 minutes, stirring every once in a while.

2. Add the peppers and chocolate and continue to simmer for 35–40 minutes, with the pan now uncovered, stirring frequently, until the sauce thickens and the chicken is falling apart. Remove from the heat and stir in the cilantro. If you are serving the chicken as it is (as a stew without the batter), it's ready to serve (or freeze, once it has come to room temperature) at this stage. If you are making the corn crust, spoon the chicken into a ceramic baking dish—one with high sides that measures about 8 x 12 inches/ 20 x 30cm—and set aside.

3. Preheat the oven to 400°F.

4. To make the batter, pour the butter into a blender with the corn, milk, egg yolks, and ¾ tsp salt. Blitz for a few seconds, to form a rough paste, then spoon into a large bowl. Place the egg whites in a separate clean bowl and whisk to form firm peaks. Fold these gently into the runny corn mixture until just combined, then pour the mix evenly over the chicken.

5. Bake for 35 minutes, until the top is golden brown. Keep an eye on it after 25 minutes to make sure the top is not taking on too much color; you might need to cover it with foil for the final 10 minutes. Remove from the oven and set aside for 10 minutes before serving.

CORN BATTER

5 tbsp/70g unsalted butter, melted

scant 4 cups/500g corn kernels, fresh or frozen and defrosted (from 4 large ears corn)

3 tbsp whole milk

3 eggs, yolks and whites separated

salt

Pictured on pages 238–239

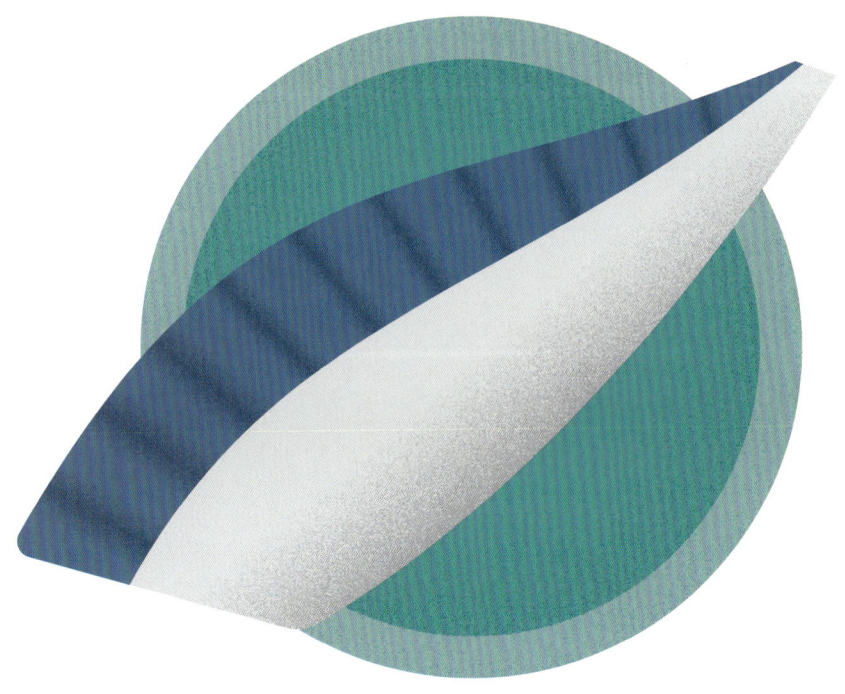

Seafood

Trout tartare with browned butter and pistachios

Tartare is all about the quality and freshness of the ingredients. The trout needs to be as fresh as can be, the nuts need to be best quality (always taste them to check for freshness), and the salt flaked. If you can get hold of them, use slivered pistachios—their long shape is very elegant and their vibrant green looks great—but regular shelled pistachios, roughly chopped, are also fine. This is as easy to make as it is impressive to serve.

1. Place the shallot in a small bowl with 2 tbsp of the lemon juice, the sugar, ½ tsp flaked salt, and a generous grind of pepper. Using your fingers, massage the sugar and salt into the shallot and set aside.

2. Put the trout in a separate small bowl along with the oil, lemon zest, the remaining 2 tsp of lemon juice, 1½ tsp flaked salt, and a generous grind of pepper. Stir and set aside for 30 minutes—not longer, or the fish will overcook.

3. Before serving, put the butter and cumin seeds into a small pan and place over medium heat. Melt the butter gently for about 5 minutes, swirling the pan from time to time, until the butter begins to foam, turn brown, smell nutty, and is caramelized.

4. Divide the trout among four dishes and top with the shallot (discarding any liquid). Sprinkle with the pistachios and tarragon and drizzle with the cumin seed–browned butter. Finish with a little sprinkle of flaked salt and serve.

Serves four as a starter

1 shallot, sliced paper-thin (5 tbsp/30g)

2 lemons: zest finely to get 2 tsp, then juice to get 2½ tbsp

½ tsp granulated sugar

flaked sea salt and black pepper

4 trout fillets, skinless, cut into ½-inch/1½cm pieces (12¾ oz/360g)

1 tsp olive oil

1½ tbsp unsalted butter

½ tsp cumin seeds

2 tbsp slivered pistachios (or roughly chopped pistachios, if you can't get any), lightly toasted

¼ cup/5g tarragon leaves, finely chopped

Mackerel with pistachio and cardamom salsa

This is a super impressive (but secretly very easy) summer starter. It also works well as a main course. Serve with some herb-filled rice.

Serves four as a starter or two as a main

8 cardamom pods (or ½ teaspoon of ground cardamom)

salt

4 mackerel fillets, skin on and pinbones removed (9¼ oz/260g)

1¼-inch/3cm piece of ginger, peeled (1 oz/25g)

2 tbsp heavy cream

2 tbsp sour cream

¾ cup/15g cilantro, finely chopped

½ cup/10g basil leaves, finely chopped

2½ tbsp shelled pistachios, lightly toasted and roughly chopped

2 limes: finely zest 1 to get 1 tsp, then juice to get 2 tsp; cut the second lime into wedges, to serve

1 green chile, seeded and finely chopped

3 tbsp/50ml sunflower oil

1. Using the flat side of a large knife, crush the cardamom pods to release the seeds. Transfer the seeds to a pestle and mortar and crush them finely; you should have about ½ tsp. Discard the pods. If starting with ground cardamom you don't need to do this.

2. Mix a pinch of cardamom (about ⅛ tsp) with a pinch of salt. Rub this on both sides of the fish and set aside until ready to fry.

3. Finely grate the ginger, then press the pulp through a sieve (with a bowl underneath); you should get 1 tsp of juice. Discard the pulp and set the liquid aside.

4. Using a fork (or a small whisk, if you have one), whip the cream until stiff. Switch to using a spatula and fold in the sour cream, ginger juice, and a small pinch of salt, so you have a soft cream. Keep in the fridge until needed.

5. Combine the cilantro and basil with the pistachios, the remaining ⅛ tsp of cardamom, the lime zest, lime juice, chile, 4 tsp/20ml of the oil, and ⅛ tsp salt. Set aside.

6. When ready to serve, put the remaining 1 tbsp plus 2 tsp of oil into a large frying pan and place over high heat. Once very hot, add the mackerel fillets, skin side down (the skin should sizzle), and fry for 2 minutes. Press the fillets with a fish spatula as they cook, to prevent the skin from curling up. Once the skin is crisp and golden brown, turn over and fry for 1 minute, until golden brown.

7. Transfer the mackerel to four individual plates. Spoon one-quarter of the ginger cream and the pistachio and cardamom salsa next to each fillet. Serve hot, with a wedge of lime.

Bridget Jones's pan-fried salmon with pine nut salsa

Serves four (halve the recipe if you're on that second date!)

¾ cup/100g currants

4 salmon fillets, skin on and pinbones removed (1 lb 2 oz/500g)

7 tbsp/100ml olive oil

salt and black pepper

4 medium celery stalks, cut into ½-inch/ 1cm dice (1¾ cups/ 180g), leaves removed but kept for garnish

¼ cup/30g pine nuts, roughly chopped

¼ cup/40g capers, plus 2 tbsp of their brine

⅓ cup/40g large green olives, pitted and cut into ½-inch/1cm dice (about 8)

1 good pinch (¼ tsp) of saffron threads, mixed with 1 tbsp hot water

1 cup/20g parsley, roughly chopped

1 lemon: finely zest to get 1 tsp, then juice to get 1 tsp

This is the dish Patrick Dempsey's character tells Renée Zellweger's Bridget Jones that he would have brought her on their imaginary second date in Bridget Jones's Baby. *"From Ottolenghi," says Dempsey, "delicious and healthy!" And easy, we might add! What sounded like a bit of product placement on our part was in fact no such thing. The recipe didn't even exist on our menu, so this is a retrospective acknowledgment.*

1. Cover the currants with boiling water and set aside to soak for 20 minutes while you prep the salmon and make the salsa.

2. Mix the salmon with 1 tbsp of the oil, a rounded ¼ tsp salt, and a good grind of pepper. Set aside while you make the salsa.

3. Put 5 tbsp/75ml of the olive oil into a large sauté pan and place on a high heat. Add the celery and pine nuts and fry for 4–5 minutes, stirring frequently, until the nuts begin to brown (don't take your eyes off them, as they can easily burn). Remove the pan from the heat and stir in the capers and their brine, the olives, saffron and its water, and a pinch of salt. Drain the currants and add these, along with the parsley, lemon zest, and lemon juice. Set aside.

4. Put the remaining 1 tbsp of oil into a large frying pan and place over medium-high heat. Once hot, add the salmon fillets, skin side down, and fry for 3 minutes, until the skin is crisp. Decrease the heat to medium, then flip the fillets over and continue to fry for 2–4 minutes (depending on how much you like the salmon cooked). Remove from the pan and set aside.

5. Arrange the salmon on four plates and spoon on the salsa. Scatter the celery leaves on top.

Roasted trout with tomato, orange, and barberry salsa

This is one of those dishes that is simple and quick enough for midweek but impressive enough to serve to guests you want to make feel special. The recipe easily doubles or triples, so that also helps. To get ahead, make the salsa the day before and keep in the fridge until ready to serve. This dish needs little more than some rice or a potato salad alongside.

Serves two

5¼ oz/150g cherry tomatoes, quartered

1 small orange: finely zest to get 1 tsp, then juice to get 1 tbsp

2 limes: juice 1 to get 1 tbsp, cut the other into wedges to serve

1½ tsp maple syrup (or honey)

1½ tbsp barberries (or currants soaked in 1 tbsp lemon juice)

1 tsp fennel seeds, lightly toasted and crushed

1 tbsp olive oil

salt and black pepper

5 tbsp/70g unsalted butter

1 small garlic clove, minced

2 whole trout, gutted and scaled (ask your fishmonger to do this for you) (1½ lb/700g)

½ cup/10g cilantro leaves, finely shredded

1. Preheat the oven to 475°F.

2. Put the tomatoes in a medium bowl with the orange zest, orange juice, lime juice, maple syrup, barberries, fennel seeds, oil, ⅛ tsp salt, and a good grind of pepper. Mix, then set aside.

3. In a small pan, gently warm the butter with the garlic over medium heat until just melted. Arrange the trout on a medium baking sheet, spaced apart. Sprinkle the top, bottom, and cavity of each fish with ¼ tsp salt. Pour the butter mixture all over the trout, making sure it covers both sides as well as the cavity. Roast in the oven for 18–20 minutes, basting once, until the fish is just cooked.

4. Serve the fish on the baking sheet or arrange on plates, spooning on some of the cooking juices. Stir the cilantro into the salsa and spoon over the fish. Serve with the lime wedges alongside.

Chile fish with tahini

Serves four

1¾ lb/800g halibut (or
  other firm white fish),
  either 4 steaks, on
  the bone, or 4 fillets,
  skinless and boneless

salt

¼ cup/60ml olive oil

1 or 2 red chiles,
  chopped crosswise into
  ¾-inch/2cm chunks,
  mostly seeded

3 garlic cloves, thinly sliced

1 tsp caraway seeds,
  plus ¼ tsp, to serve

1 ancho chile, trimmed,
  seeded and torn into
  2-inch/5cm pieces (or 1 tsp
  sweet smoked paprika)

**2 lb 2 oz/1kg plum
  tomatoes,** chopped
  into ½-inch/1cm dice

¼ cup/50g tomato paste

½ tsp granulated sugar

¼ cup/5g cilantro leaves,
  roughly chopped, to serve

TAHINI SAUCE

3 tbsp tahini

1 tbsp lemon juice

¼ cup/60 ml water

salt

*There are very few things, in my book, that aren't improved by a drizzle
of creamy tahini sauce. Here it makes perfect sense, balancing the
chile and bringing a welcome creaminess.*

*I tend to make double the tomato sauce and keep the excess in
the fridge for 1 week, or the freezer for 1 month, so you can either
make this dish twice or spoon it alongside some grilled chicken or veg.
The tahini sauce can be made 3 days ahead and kept in the fridge.*

1. Lightly season the fish with a rounded ¼ tsp of salt. Set aside.

2. Put the oil into a large sauté pan with a lid and place over
medium-high heat. Once hot, add the red chiles and fry for
2 minutes, stirring frequently. Add the garlic, caraway seeds,
and ancho, and continue to fry for 1 minute, until the garlic is
starting to turn golden brown. Add the tomatoes, tomato paste,
sugar, and ½ tsp salt, then, once boiling, decrease the heat
to medium and let simmer for 15 minutes, stirring from time to
time, until the sauce is thick. Add the fish, cover the pan, and
continue to cook for 10 minutes.

3. To make the tahini sauce, mix the tahini and lemon juice with
the water and ⅛ tsp salt.

4. When ready to serve, gently lift the fish out of the pan and
set aside somewhere warm. If the fish has released a lot of liquid
during the cooking and the sauce is runny, increase the heat and
let it bubble away quickly until thick. Taste and add salt if needed.

5. Transfer the fish to a serving dish. Spoon on the sauce, sprinkle
with the cilantro, and serve.

Coconut-crusted fish fingers

Serves four

**1 lb 2 oz/500g skinless
and boneless haddock**
(or other firm white fish),
cut into about 12 pieces,
each 1¼ x 4 inches/
3 x 10cm

2 tbsp lime juice

**¼ cup/60ml coconut
cream**

salt

**7 oz/200g fresh coconut
flesh** (from 1 medium
coconut), coarsely
grated (or 2 cups/
150g dried unsweetened
shredded coconut)

**⅓ cup/20g panko
breadcrumbs**

**1 tsp crushed red
pepper flakes**

**¼ cup/60g unsalted
butter,** melted

1 lime, quartered, to serve

*This makes a welcome change to the fish finger theme for kids who
love this alternative. The pepper flakes aren't too hot but reduce or
lose them if they're going to put anyone off. Thanks to Jamie Kirkaldy
for giving Esme the idea to make these.*

1. Place the fish in a bowl with the lime juice, coconut cream,
and ¼ tsp salt. Mix, then leave in the fridge for about 1 hour, to
marinate (don't leave it for much longer than that, as the fish will
start to disintegrate). Scrape off and discard as much of the cream
as you can from the fish, then set aside.

2. Place a large frying pan over medium-high heat and, once hot,
add the coconut. Dry-fry for 6–7 minutes (or just 2–3 minutes,
if using dried), stirring from time to time, until golden. Transfer
to a medium shallow bowl and set aside to cool, then mix in the
panko, pepper flakes, and ½ tsp salt.

3. When ready to cook, preheat your broiler to high.

4. Coating one at a time, dip a piece of fish into the melted butter,
followed by the coconut mix. Toss until it is coated on all sides and
transfer to a wire rack placed on top of a large parchment-lined
baking sheet. Continue with the remaining fish pieces.

5. Place under the broiler on the center oven rack—otherwise it
will burn!—and cook for 5–6 minutes, turning the pieces carefully
after 2–3 minutes, until cooked through and golden brown. If the
fish is not cooked but the coating is brown and ready, just turn
off the broiler and leave in the oven for 2–3 minutes; the fish will
cook in the residual heat. Serve with the lime wedges.

Fish cake tacos with mango, lime, and cumin yogurt

*Makes twelve tacos,
to serve four*

**15¾ oz/450g plaice
fillets** (or a similar
white fish), skin and
pinbones removed,
cut into ¾–1¼-inch/
2–3cm chunks

1 garlic clove, crushed

1 large egg

1½ tsp cumin seeds,
toasted and finely
crushed in a pestle
and mortar

4 limes: finely zest to get
1 tbsp, then cut into
wedges, to serve

salt

**1 cup/20g cilantro
leaves,** finely chopped

**½ cup/120g Greek-style
yogurt**

½ red onion, thinly sliced
(½ cup/40g)

½ mango, peeled and
julienned (½ cup/100g)

1 red chile, seeded and
julienned (1 tbsp)

3 tbsp vegetable oil

**12 (6-inch/15cm) corn
or flour tortillas,**
warmed through

Making tacos is a really easy and fun way to feed friends. You can prepare everything well in advance—the fish cake mixture (uncooked), the yogurt, and the onion and mango pickle can all be made a day ahead and kept separate in the fridge—then just hop to the stove 5 minutes before everyone wants to eat, cook the fish cakes, and heat the tortillas. Reheat any leftovers the next day. The dish also works well without the tortillas, if you want to eat with a knife and fork.

1. Place the fish, garlic, and egg in the large bowl of a food processor with 1 tsp of the cumin seeds, 1 tsp of the lime zest, and ¾ tsp salt. Blitz briefly, just until the fish forms a coarse paste, then transfer to a medium bowl. Add ½ cup of the cilantro, mix, then form into 12 round fish cakes, each weighing about 1½ oz/45g. Refrigerate for at least 15 minutes (and up to 1 day ahead), to firm up.

2. Put the yogurt, the remaining ½ tsp of the cumin seeds, the remaining lime zest, and ⅛ tsp salt into a small bowl. Mix together and set aside.

3. In a separate small bowl, combine the onion, mango, and chile and set aside.

4. Heat the oil in a large nonstick frying pan and place over medium-high heat. Once the oil is hot, add the fish cakes in batches and fry for 2–3 minutes on each side, until golden brown and cooked through. Transfer to a paper towel–lined plate.

5. Serve each taco warm, with 1 fish cake, cut in half, a spoonful of yogurt, and the mango mix. Finish with a sprinkle of the remaining ½ cup of cilantro and a squeeze of lime.

Smoked fish and parsnip cakes

I love to eat these for brunch, topped with a poached egg, but they're good at any time of the day. If eating them for lunch or supper, try grating some fresh horseradish into sour cream to serve alongside. I've allowed for two cakes each, but some people will prefer one, particularly if eating them in the morning topped with an egg. The patties can be made up to 24 hours before serving, up to the point of frying, and kept in the fridge.

1. Preheat the oven to 400°F.

2. Toss the parsnips with 3 tbsp of the oil and ¼ tsp of salt. Transfer to a large parchment-lined baking pan and roast for 30 minutes, until golden brown and soft. Tip into a food processor and blitz to form a coarse mash. If the mix is very dry, then add the water and blitz again to combine. Transfer to a large bowl and set aside.

3. Place the fish in the food processor (don't worry about wiping it clean) and pulse a few times—you want it to be roughly chopped rather than completely minced—then add to the bowl of parsnips, along with the dill, chives, garlic, lemon zest, eggs, 1 tsp salt, and plenty of pepper. Mix well, then form into 12 patties; they should be about 3¼ inch/8cm wide and ¾–1¼ inches/2–3cm thick. At this stage you can cover the patties and keep them in the fridge until ready to cook (up to 24 hours).

4. Put 1½ tbsp of the butter and 2½ tbsp of the remaining oil into a large frying pan and place over medium-high heat. Once the butter starts to foam, add half the patties and fry for 8 minutes, turning them after 4 minutes, until crisp and golden brown. Keep warm while you cook the rest, adding the remaining 1½ tbsp of butter and 2½ tbsp of oil to the pan. Serve with wedges of lemon.

Makes twelve cakes,
to serve six

6 parsnips, peeled and
 cut into 1½-inch/4cm
 chunks (6 cups/600g)
½ cup/120ml olive oil
salt
1–2 tbsp water,
 as needed
1 lb 3¾ oz/560g
 smoked cod or
 haddock fillets,
 skinless and boneless,
 chopped into 1½-inch/
 4cm pieces
1 cup/20g dill, roughly
 chopped
1 cup/20g chives,
 roughly chopped
2 garlic cloves, minced
2 lemons: finely zest to
 get 2 tsp, then cut into
 wedges, to serve
2 large eggs, lightly
 beaten
black pepper
3 tbsp unsalted butter

Grilled prawn, corn, and tomato salad

Serves four as a starter
or two as a main

DRESSING

¾-inch/2cm piece of
   ginger, peeled and
   finely chopped (2 tbsp)

1 tbsp sriracha

1½ tbsp olive oil

1 lime: finely zest to
   get 1 tsp, then juice
   to get 1½ tbsp

¼ tsp granulated sugar

salt

15½ oz/440g shell-on
   tiger prawns, peeled
   and deveined, tail
   on (or peeled tiger
   prawns) (8½ oz/240g)

1 tsp olive oil

salt

1 small red onion,
   cut into ½-inch/
   1½cm wedges
   (mounded 1 cup/120g)

¾ cup/100g frozen
   corn, defrosted

9 oz/250g cherry
   tomatoes

1 tbsp marjoram leaves
   (or oregano)

Taking the shell off the prawns can be a bit of a fiddly job, so start with peeled prawns (fresh, or frozen and defrosted), if you like. They won't have the tail intact, which always looks great, but they work perfectly well. If you want to get ahead, make the dressing up to 2 days in advance.

1. To make the dressing, mix together the ginger, sriracha, olive oil, lime, sugar, and ⅛ tsp salt. Set aside.

2. Place a grill pan over high heat and ventilate your kitchen well. While the grill pan is heating up, mix the shrimp with the oil and ⅛ tsp salt and set aside. Place the onion on the grill pan for 5 minutes, turning over every so often until charred and cooked but still retaining a bite. Transfer to a large bowl, then add the corn to the grill pan. Cook for 2 minutes, until charred, then add to the onion.

3. Continue with the tomatoes, adding them to the grill pan for 3 minutes, turning throughout so that they are charred on all sides. Add to the bowl of onion and corn. Add the shrimp to the grill pan and grill for 4 minutes, turning after 2 minutes, until the shrimp are charred and cooked through. Add to the vegetables, along with the marjoram and the dressing. Gently stir to combine and serve.

Squid and red bell pepper stew

This is a one-pot dish, big on flavor, which simmers away for just 30 minutes while you get on with something else in the kitchen. It's also delicious a day or two after you make it—just keep in the fridge and warm through before serving. Serve with plain couscous or rice, or just some crusty bread to soak up the juices, along with a crisp green salad. Ask your fishmonger to clean the fresh squid for you, if you don't want to do it yourself; otherwise bags of frozen (and cleaned) squid are widely available.

1. Put the oil into a large sauté pan with a lid and place over medium-high heat. Add the onion and bell pepper, along with a rounded ¼ tsp salt, and cook for 5 minutes, stirring from time to time. Add the garlic, caraway seeds, allspice, and a really good grind of black pepper. Continue to sauté for another 5 minutes, until everything is nice and soft.

2. Add the squid, cook for 5 minutes, then stir in the tomato paste, bay leaves, and thyme. Cook for another 2–3 minutes, then pour in the wine. Decrease the heat to low and allow everything to simmer away, covered, for about 30 minutes, stirring a few times, until the squid is cooked and soft. If the sauce is turning dry toward the end of cooking, you might need to add 1–2 tbsp of water. Add the orange zest just before serving and give everything a final gentle stir.

Serves two as a main or four as part of a tapas spread

5 tbsp/70ml olive oil

1 medium onion, sliced into thick pinwheels, about ½ inch/1cm wide (1⅔ cups/160g)

1 large red bell pepper, halved, cored, seeded, and sliced lengthwise ½ inch/1cm thick (2 cups/150g)

salt

2 garlic cloves, thinly sliced

2 tsp caraway seeds

¾ tsp ground allspice

black pepper

2 lb 2 oz/1kg squid, cleaned, skin removed, cut into ½-inch/1½cm strips (1 lb 2 oz/500g)

1½ tbsp tomato paste

3 bay leaves

1 tbsp chopped thyme leaves

10 tbsp/150ml red wine

1 small orange, finely zested to get ¼ tsp (optional)

Whole roasted sea bass with soy sauce and ginger

This is the centerpiece for an Asian-style feast, served with some Thai sticky rice (page 173) and Broccolini with soy sauce, garlic, and peanuts (page 76) or any other green. If you want to get ahead, the fish can be prepared a few hours in advance and kept in the fridge, ready for the sauce to be poured on top and the dish placed in the oven. Thanks to Helen Goh.

Serves four

SAUCE

7 tbsp/100ml chicken stock (or vegetable stock)

2 tbsp sesame oil

2 tbsp shaoxing wine (or dry sherry)

3½ tbsp light soy sauce

1 tbsp granulated sugar

1 whole sea bass, about 18 inches/45cm long, scaled, gutted and rinsed (2 lb 2 oz/1kg)

flaked sea salt

10 green onions, trimmed (5¾ oz/160g)

1 medium 1 lb 10 oz/ 750g green cabbage, halved, cored and leaves removed individually

1½-inch/4cm piece of ginger, peeled and julienned (¼ cup/30g)

1 red chile, seeded and julienned

5 tbsp/75ml peanut oil

½ cup/10g cilantro leaves, or leaves and stems, if tender

1. Preheat the oven to 425°F.

2. Put all the ingredients for the sauce in a small pan and place over high heat. Once boiling, cook for 1 minute, swirling the pan slightly so that the sugar dissolves. Remove from the heat and set aside.

3. Make 5 diagonal slits on both sides of the fish, ¼ inch/½cm deep and about 3¼ inches/8cm long. Sprinkle 1 tsp of flaked salt evenly over one side of the fish and rub in. Repeat with another tsp on the other side, then sprinkle the inside with another ½ tsp. Cut 8 of the green onions into 2-inch/5cm lengths and set aside. Thinly slice the remaining 2 green onions and set aside, keeping them separate.

4. Spread the cabbage and larger pieces of green onions out into a large baking dish or pan. Place the fish diagonally on top and sprinkle with the ginger. Pour the sauce over the fish, then cover the pan tightly with foil and place in the oven for 40 minutes, basting twice during the process, until it is cooked through. To check that it is ready, gently insert a knife into one of the slits and check that the flesh comes away from the bones and is opaque. Sprinkle with the thinly sliced green onion, along with the chile, and set aside.

5. Pour the peanut oil into a small pan and place over high heat for about 2 minutes, until it starts to smoke. Very carefully pour it evenly over the fish so that the skin and vegetables start to crisp. Top with the cilantro and serve, either straight from the baking dish or on a platter. If on a platter, arrange the cabbage leaves and green onion on the platter—pull them out from under the fish—then carefully lift the fish to sit on top. Pour the cooking sauce on top and serve.

Rose harissa chickpeas with flaked cod

Serves four as a tapas or side

7 oz/200g cod, skinless and boneless, cut into 1¼-inch/3cm pieces

2½ tbsp olive oil

rounded ¼ tsp ground cumin

2 garlic cloves, 1 minced and 1 thinly sliced

salt

½ onion, finely chopped (¾ cup/100g)

2 cardamom pods, bashed with the flat side of a knife

1 tbsp rose harissa (or 50 percent more or less, depending on variety; see page 301)

2 tsp tomato paste

1½ small preserved lemons, skin finely chopped (3 tbsp)

1 (15.5 oz/440g) can chickpeas, drained and rinsed (1¾ cups/240g)

¾ cup plus 2 tbsp/ 200ml vegetable stock

¼ cup/5g cilantro, roughly chopped

This is a great little tapas dish packed full of big flavors. Serve it with some crusty bread and wilted greens.

1. Mix the cod with 1½ tsp of the olive oil, the cumin, crushed garlic, and ⅛ tsp salt. Set aside for 15 minutes to marinate.

2. Put the remaining 2 tbsp of oil in a large sauté pan and place over medium heat. Once hot, add the onion and fry for 4–5 minutes, stirring frequently, until soft and golden brown. Decrease the heat to medium, add the sliced garlic, and stir for 1 minute, then add the cardamom, harissa, tomato paste, preserved lemon, chickpeas, and ¼ tsp salt. Stir for 1 minute, then add the stock and heat for 3–4 minutes, crushing some of the chickpeas with the back of a spoon, until the sauce is thick.

3. Add the fish to the pan and cook for 3–4 minutes, stirring gently and turning the fish after 1½–2 minutes, until cooked and flaking apart. Lift out and discard the cardamom pods, sprinkle with the cilantro, spoon into shallow bowls, and serve.

Pictured on pages 264–265

Shrimp and corn fritters

These fritters work as both a snack before supper and as a starter with an avocado and gem lettuce salad. They also work in bite-sized form, as a canapé. Just make them one-third of the size and decrease the cooking time to 1 minute on each side. The mix can be made up the day before, if you want to get ahead, and then just wait in the fridge to be fried. You can also fry them the day before, if you like, and keep them in the fridge, warming through before serving.

1. Put the shrimp and corn in the bowl of a food processor and give them a quick pulse to break them up. Add the cumin, coriander, paprika, pepper flakes, cilantro, egg, lime zest, and a rounded ¼ tsp of salt and pulse a few more times, until the shrimp are roughly broken and the ingredients are mixed together. Spoon into a bowl and set aside.

2. Put the oil in a medium frying pan and place over medium-high heat. Once hot, use 2 spoons to form half of the mixture into 6 fritters (or more, if making canapé size). Put them into the pan and flatten slightly so they are about ¾ inch/2cm thick. Fry for 2 minutes on each side (or 1 minute on each side if making the smaller version), then transfer to a paper towel–lined plate.

3. Continue with the remaining mixture in the same way and serve warm, with a sprinkle of salt and the wedges of lime.

Makes twelve fritters, to serve six as a starter or snack or about thirty-six bite-size fritters, to serve twelve as a canapé

12¼ oz/350g peeled jumbo shrimp

mounded 1 cup/140g frozen corn, defrosted

¼ tsp ground cumin

½ tsp ground coriander

½ tsp smoked paprika

¼ tsp crushed red pepper flakes

½ cup/10g cilantro, roughly chopped

1 large egg, beaten

2 limes: finely zest to get 2 tsp, then cut into wedges, to serve

salt

3 tbsp vegetable oil

Pictured on pages 264–265

Dessert

Sweet and salty cheesecake with cherries

There are three components here—I know, but they're all quick and simple to do, can all be made well in advance, and there's no work to do on the day you're serving apart from some informal assembly. The cheesecake (which keeps for 3 days) and compote (which keeps for 5 days) need to be kept in the fridge, and the crumble (which keeps a good week or so) just needs to be kept in an airtight container at room temperature. The compote and crumble are also lovely for breakfast—if you have any left over or want to make more—served with Greek yogurt.

Serves six to eight

3½ oz/100g **feta**

10 oz/300g **full-fat cream cheese,** at room temperature

3 tbsp **granulated sugar**

1 small **lemon,** finely zested to get 1 tsp

½ cup plus 1 tbsp/ 130ml **heavy cream**

CRUMBLE

¾ cup/100g **blanched hazelnuts,** roughly chopped

2 tbsp **unsalted butter,** fridge-cold and cut into ¾-inch/2cm dice

⅔ cup/80g **almond meal**

2 tbsp/25g **granulated sugar**

1 tbsp **black sesame seeds** (or white)

⅛ tsp **salt**

CHERRY COMPOTE

1 lb 5 oz/600g **frozen pitted cherries,** defrosted

7 tbsp/90g **granulated sugar**

4 whole **star anise**

1 **orange:** peel finely shaved to get 4 strips

2 tbsp **olive oil,** to serve

1. Using a spatula, break the feta down in a large bowl to make it as smooth as possible. Add the cream cheese, sugar, and lemon zest and whisk to combine. Pour in the cream and gently whisk until the mixture has thickened enough to hold its shape. Leave to set in the fridge until ready to use.

2. Preheat the oven to 400°F.

3. To make the crumble, place the hazelnuts, butter, almond meal, and sugar in a bowl. Use the tips of your fingers to rub the butter into everything else until the consistency of breadcrumbs is formed. Stir in the sesame seeds and salt, then spread out on a baking sheet. Bake for about 12 minutes, until golden brown.

4. To make the compote, put the cherries, sugar, star anise, and orange peel into a medium saucepan and place over medium-high heat. Bring to a boil, then simmer for 10–15 minutes, until the sauce has thickened (but it will continue to thicken as it cools down). Set aside to come to room temperature. Discard star anise and orange peel.

5. When ready to serve, spoon a large scoop of the cheesecake into each bowl and top with some crumble. Spoon the compote on top and finish with the remaining crumble. Drizzle with the olive oil and serve.

Vanilla custard with roasted strawberries and rhubarb

If it's in season, use forced rhubarb here: the hot-pink color of the slender stalks looks stunning once cooked. Regular field-grown rhubarb, though, is also great. The custard and fruit mixtures can be made a day in advance and kept in the fridge until ready to assemble. Serve this with some shortbread alongside, if you're looking for crunch.

1. Preheat the oven to 425°F.

2. Mix the rhubarb and strawberries with the sugar and arrange in a medium ovenproof dish; you want the fruit to fit snugly. Bake for 12–13 minutes, until the fruit has softened but still retains its shape and the sugar has melted. Don't worry if there is a tiny amount of sugar that hasn't melted; just give the fruit a gentle stir and the sugar will dissolve. Set aside to cool.

3. Decrease the oven temperature to 375°F.

4. For the custard, place the egg yolks, cornstarch, sugar, and vanilla in a large bowl and whisk until smooth. Gradually pour in the cream and whisk until combined. Pour the custard into a 10-inch/25cm high-sided ovenproof dish. Place the dish inside a larger ovenproof dish and fill the larger dish with boiling water so it rises about ½-inch/1cm up the sides. Bake for 25 minutes, until the custard has set and is starting to brown on top. Remove from the oven, set aside to cool, then transfer to the fridge to chill.

5. Once chilled, spoon half of the fruit and juice on top and serve with the remaining fruit and juice alongside.

Serves eight to ten

7 oz/200g rhubarb, cut into 1¼-inch/ 3cm chunks

7 oz/200g strawberries, hulled and halved lengthwise

7 tbsp/90g granulated sugar

CUSTARD

4 large egg yolks

1 tsp cornstarch

rounded ¼ cup/60g granulated sugar

2 tsp vanilla extract

2½ cups/600ml heavy cream

Sumac-roasted strawberries with yogurt cream

Serves six

3¾ cups/900g Greek-style yogurt

1 cup plus 3 tbsp/140g confectioners' sugar

salt

½ cup/120ml heavy cream

1 lemon: finely zest to get 1 tsp, then juice to get 2 tbsp

⅓ cup/80 ml water

1 lb 5 oz/600g ripe strawberries, hulled and halved lengthwise

1½ tbsp sumac

½ cup/10g mint, half sprigs and the other half leaves, finely shredded

1 vanilla pod, split lengthwise and seeds scraped

⅓ cup/80ml water

This is a good dessert if you have overripe strawberries that are slightly past their best. Roasting them makes them deliciously soft and sticky. All of the elements can be made 3 days in advance—keep them separate in the fridge and assemble when ready to serve. Serve this as it is, for a light summer dessert, or with shortbread biscuits. Thanks to Helen Graham.

1. Put the yogurt in a bowl with ½ cup plus 4½ tsp confectioners' sugar and ¼ tsp salt. Mix, then transfer to a sieve lined with cheesecloth and set over a bowl. Tie the cheesecloth into a bundle with string, weight it down with a heavy bowl, and refrigerate for 30 minutes. Extract as much liquid as possible, until you are left with about 2 cups plus 5 tbsp/550g of thickened yogurt. Remove from the cheesecloth—discarding any liquid—and transfer to a bowl. Stir in the cream and lemon zest and refrigerate until ready to use.

2. Preheat the oven to 425°F.

3. Meanwhile, roast the strawberries. Toss the strawberries with the sumac, mint sprigs, vanilla pod and seeds, lemon juice, the remaining confectioners' sugar, and the water. Transfer to an ovenproof dish measuring about 8 x 12 inches/20 x 30cm. Roast for 20 minutes, tossing after 10 minutes, until soft and bubbling. Let cool to room temperature, then lift out and discard the mint and vanilla pod. Strain the roasting juices into a jug. Pour 3 tbsp of the juices into the yogurt cream and gently fold it through so the cream is rippled. Set aside 3 tbsp of juices to serve. (Keep the remaining juices to drizzle over your morning granola.)

4. To serve, spoon the rippled cream into bowls and top with the strawberries. Pour the juices over the top and garnish with the shredded mint.

Plum, blackberry, and bay friand

Serves six generously

7 oz/200g blackberries

4 ripe plums, pits removed, cut into ½-inch/1cm wedges (2½ cups/360g)

1 tsp vanilla extract

rounded ¼ cup/60g granulated sugar

3 fresh bay leaves

1 tsp ground cinnamon

6 tbsp/60g all-purpose flour

1⅔ cups/200g confectioners' sugar, sifted

1 cup/120g almond meal

⅛ tsp salt

5¼ oz/150g egg whites (from 4 or 5 large eggs)

¾ cup/180g unsalted butter, melted and slightly cooled

Friands are the light, moist almond cakes popular in Australia, New Zealand, and France. Whisked egg whites and very little flour make them wonderfully light, and the almond meal makes them really moist. Traditionally they're small cakes, but here I tip the batter into a baking dish and cook it whole.

You can make the batter well in advance, if you want to get ahead—it keeps well in the fridge up to 1 day. But don't macerate the fruit for this amount of time as it will become too juicy.

Serve with custard, vanilla ice cream, or whipped cream. The fruit can be played around with, depending on the season. Raspberries and peaches can be used in the early summer months, for example.

1. Place the blackberries and plums in a bowl with the vanilla, granulated sugar, bay leaves, and ½ tsp of the cinnamon. Set aside for 30 minutes. Don't be tempted to leave them sitting around for longer than this, as the fruit will become too juicy.

2. Preheat the oven to 400°F.

3. Mix the flour, confectioners' sugar, almond meal, the remaining ½ tsp of cinnamon, and salt in a separate large bowl. Set aside.

4. Lightly whisk the egg whites by hand for 30 seconds, so they just start to froth. Stir into the flour mixture, along with the melted butter, until combined.

5. Tip the batter into a 9 x 13-inch/23 x 33cm parchment-lined baking dish and top evenly with the fruit and juices. Bake for 60 minutes, covering the dish with foil for the final 10 minutes, until the cake is golden brown and the fruit is bubbling. Set aside for 10 minutes before serving.

Blueberry, almond, and lemon cake

Serves eight

½ cup plus 2 tbsp/150g unsalted butter, at room temperature

1 cup/190g granulated sugar

2 lemons: finely zest to get 2 tsp, then juice to get 2 tbsp

1 tsp vanilla extract

3 large eggs, beaten

⅔ cup/90g all-purpose flour, sifted

½ tsp baking powder

⅛ tsp salt

¾ cup plus 2 tbsp/110g almond meal

7 oz/200g blueberries

½ cup plus 1 tbsp/70g confectioners' sugar

For all the pans and molds that can be used to great effect in baking, there's nothing quite like a simple loaf cake to reassure one that all is okay with the world. This is timeless, easy, and also keeps well, for 3 days, stored in an airtight container at room temperature.

1. Preheat the oven to 400°F. Grease an 8½ x 4½-inch/21 x 11cm loaf pan, and line the base with parchment paper.

2. Place the butter, granulated sugar, lemon zest, 1 tbsp of the lemon juice, and vanilla in the bowl of a stand mixer fitted with the paddle attachment. Beat on high speed for 3–4 minutes, until light, then lower the speed to medium. Add the eggs, in small additions, scraping down the sides of the bowl. The mix may separate a little, but don't worry; it'll come back together. Add the flour, salt, baking powder, and almond meal in three additions. Finally, fold in three-quarters of the blueberries, scrape into the prepared loaf pan, and smooth it out evenly.

3. Bake for 15 minutes, then sprinkle the remaining blueberries over the top of the cake. Return to the oven for another 15 minutes, until the cake is golden brown but still uncooked. Cover loosely with foil and continue to bake for 25–30 minutes, until risen and cooked. Test by inserting a knife into the middle; it's ready if it comes out clean. Remove from the oven and set aside, in its pan, to cool for 10 minutes, then remove from the pan and place on a wire rack to cool completely.

4. Meanwhile, make the icing. Put the remaining 1 tbsp of lemon juice into a bowl with the confectioners' sugar and whisk until smooth. Pour over the cake and gently spread out—the blueberries on the top of the cake will bleed into the icing a little, but don't worry; this will add to the finished look.

Fig and thyme clafoutis

Serves four

7 tbsp/90g dark
   muscovado sugar

1 tbsp water

2 tbsp red wine

1 tbsp thyme leaves

2 lemons: finely zest
   to get 2 tsp, then
   juice to get 1 tbsp

14¾ oz/420g really ripe
   Mission figs (about 10,
   depending on size),
   tough stems removed,
   halved lengthwise

2 large eggs, yolks and
   whites separated

⅓ cup/50g all-purpose
   flour

1½ tsp vanilla extract

7 tbsp/100ml heavy
   cream

⅛ tsp salt

vanilla ice cream
   (or crème fraîche,
   to serve)

This might seem like a lot to serve four, but it's so light and fluffy that you'll be surprised how much everyone can eat. The figs can be made 2 days ahead and kept in the fridge.

1. Preheat the oven to 375°F.

2. Put 4 tbsp/50g of the sugar into a small ovenproof high-sided sauté pan (about 7 inches/18cm), along with the water. (If you don't have an ovenproof pan this size, cook the figs in a regular frying pan and transfer them to a 9-inch/22cm baking dish.) Place over medium-high heat for 3–4 minutes, swirling the pan a few times, until the sugar has completely melted and is bubbling rapidly. Carefully add the wine and thyme and stir continuously for about 1 minute, keeping the pan on the heat, until combined and thick. Remove from the heat, stir in the lemon juice and figs, and set aside to cool for 20 minutes (or longer)—you just don't want them to be piping hot when the topping gets poured on. If you need to transfer the figs to a baking dish, do this now.

3. Place the egg yolks in a bowl with the remaining 3 tbsp/40g of sugar, the flour, vanilla, cream, lemon zest, and salt. Whisk until pale and thickened: 2–3 minutes by hand, or 1 minute with a handheld mixer. Whisk the egg whites separately by hand for 1–2 minutes, to form stiff peaks, and fold gently into the batter until just combined.

4. Spread out the figs in the sauté pan (or baking dish) and pour in the batter. Bake for 30 minutes, until the batter has risen and is golden brown and cooked through. Remove from the oven, divide among four bowls, and serve hot with the ice cream or crème fraîche.

Honey and yogurt set cheesecake

No oven, no bain-marie, no cracks—this is the simplest of cheesecakes! You can make this up to 2 days ahead, topping with the honey and thyme just before serving if you like. It will keep in the fridge but the base will soften with time.

Serves eight

2 cups plus 2 tbsp/500g Greek-style yogurt

About 12 (7 oz/200g) Hobnobs (or other oat-flour cookie)

¼ cup/60g unsalted butter, melted

1½ tbsp thyme leaves

14 oz/400g cream cheese, at room temperature

¼ cup plus 1 tbsp/ 40g confectioners' sugar, sifted

1 lemon, finely zested to get 1 tsp

5¼ oz/150g white chocolate, broken into ½–¾-inch/ 1–2cm pieces

3 tbsp/60g honey

1. Line a 9-inch/23cm springform cake pan with parchment paper and set aside.

2. Line a sieve with a clean kitchen towel and set above a bowl. Spoon in the yogurt, then draw up the sides of the kitchen towel. Squeeze the yogurt into a ball, pressing out as much liquid as you can. You want to end up with about 1⅔ cups/340g of thickened yogurt. Set aside until required. Discard the liquid.

3. Place the Hobnobs in a clean plastic bag and crush them finely with a rolling pin. Mix with the

butter and 1 tbsp of the thyme and spoon into the cake pan, pressing it down to form an even layer. Set aside in the fridge.

4. Whisk together the cream cheese, strained yogurt, confectioners' sugar, and lemon zest until smooth and combined; this can be done in a stand mixer or using a handheld mixer.

5. Next melt the chocolate. This needs to be done in a heatproof bowl set over a pan of barely simmering water (taking care that the base of the bowl is not touching the water). Stir the chocolate frequently for 2–3 minutes, taking care not to get any moisture into the chocolate as this will cause it to seize. Spoon the melted chocolate into the cream cheese mixture and whisk until combined.

6. Spread the cream cheese mixture over the cookie base evenly, then refrigerate for at least 2 hours, until set.

7. When ready to serve, warm the honey in a small saucepan with the remaining 1½ tsp of thyme leaves until thin and runny. Remove from the heat and drizzle over the cheesecake.

8. Release the cheesecake from the pan, divide into 8 slices, and serve.

Hazelnut, peach, and raspberry cake

I like to use blanched hazelnuts to keep the cake light in color, but unskinned work just as well, if that's what you have—the color of the cake will just be darker. The cake tastes great when it is still slightly warm, but it's also fine at room temperature. It will keep for 1 day in an airtight container, but (as with all cakes made with hazelnuts, which tend to dry out quickly) not much longer.

1. Preheat the oven to 375°F. Line a 9-inch/24cm round springform cake pan with parchment paper and brush with the oil.

2. Place the peaches in a medium bowl with 1½ cups/150g of the raspberries and 1 tbsp of the sugar. Mix and set aside.

3. Put the hazelnuts into a food processor and blitz for under 1 minute, until roughly ground. Set aside.

4. Put the remaining 1½ cups plus 1 tbsp/310g sugar and the butter into the bowl of a standing mixer fitted with the paddle attachment. Beat until smooth and well combined, then gradually add the eggs, mixing until incorporated. Add the ground hazelnuts, flour, baking powder, and salt and continue to mix until smooth. Spread the batter evenly in the cake pan and arrange the peach slices and raspberries randomly on top. Bake for 70–80 minutes, covering the cake with foil after 30 minutes so that it does not take on too much color.

5. Remove from the oven and set aside to cool slightly before releasing the cake from its pan. Place the remaining ½ cup/50g of raspberries on top of the cake, in the middle, and serve.

Serves ten

2 tsp sunflower oil

2 large peaches, pits removed, sliced into ½-inch/1½cm wedges (2½ cups/340g)

2 cups/200g raspberries

1½ cups plus 2 tbsp/ 320g granulated sugar

1 cup/125g blanched hazelnuts

¾ cup plus 2 tbsp/ 200g unsalted butter, at room temperature

3 large eggs, beaten

¾ cup plus 2 tbsp/ 125g all-purpose flour

1½ tsp baking powder

⅛ tsp salt

Spiced apple cake

This can either be eaten as it is, slightly warm or at room temperature, served with or without a scoop of vanilla ice cream. This cake should be eaten on the day it is baked, or the day after; store in an airtight container to keep it at its best.

1. Preheat the oven to 350°F. Grease a high-sided 9-inch/23cm cake pan and line the base and sides with parchment paper.

2. Place the butter and granulated sugar in the bowl of a stand mixer fitted with the paddle attachment. Beat on medium speed, until light and fluffy. Add the eggs and vanilla, a little at a time, mixing until incorporated. Sift together the flour, baking powder, and salt and add this in a couple of batches to the batter, alternating with the sour cream. Turn the machine off as soon as everything is incorporated. Spoon the batter into the cake pan and set aside.

3. Place all the apple slices in a large bowl. Mix the demerara sugar and apple pie spice and sprinkle over the apples. Toss to coat, then spoon over the cake batter. Bake for 60–65 minutes, until the mixture has risen up around the apple and the top is crisp, firm, and golden brown. A knife inserted into the cake will not come out clean, as the apples are wet, but you can tell the cake is done when you give the pan a little shake and the top doesn't wobble.

4. Remove from the oven and set aside for about 30 minutes before removing from the pan.

5. Serve either slightly warm or at room temperature. When slicing, use a serrated knife to prevent the apples from tearing.

Serves ten

½ **cup plus 1½ tbsp/ 130g unsalted butter,** at room temperature and cubed

¾ **cup/150g granulated sugar**

3 large eggs, lightly beaten

2 tsp vanilla extract

2 cups plus 2 tbsp/ 300g all-purpose flour

1 tbsp baking powder

rounded ¼ tsp salt

¾ **cup/200g sour cream**

APPLE TOPPING

3–4 large Granny Smith apples, peeled, cored and cut into ½-inch/1½cm wedges (3¾ cups/590g)

⅔ **cup/130g demerara sugar**

1 tbsp apple pie spice

Nutella, sesame, and hazelnut rolls

Two assumptions qualify these for Ottolenghi SIMPLE: one is that everyone has a jar of Nutella in their cupboard (hence "P" for pantry-led—a bit of a stretch we know!) and second, for the "E," that making your own dough and rolling it up into all sorts of deliciousness is easier than it looks. The result is something between a cake and a cookie, best enjoyed as a treat with a cup of tea or coffee. The dough is delicate so it's important that you soften the Nutella (until it's nearly runny) before spreading it. Inspired by a similar pastry served at Landwer Cafe in Tel Aviv.

Makes ten rolls

I cup plus 3 tbsp/150g bread flour, plus a little extra to dust the work surface

¾ tsp fast-acting instant dried yeast

1½ tsp granulated sugar

3 tbsp olive oil, plus a little extra for greasing

¼ tsp salt

brimming ¼ cup/65ml lukewarm water

mounded ¼ cup/40g blanched hazelnuts, toasted and roughly chopped

2 tbsp sesame seeds, lightly toasted

½ cup/150g Nutella, softened (in the microwave or gently on the stove, until easily spreadable)

I small orange, finely zested to get 1 tsp

2 tsp confectioners' sugar

I. Put the flour, yeast, sugar, 2 tbsp of the oil, and the salt into a large bowl and mix to combine. Gently pour in the water, then, using a spatula, bring the mixture

together until combined. Transfer to a lightly oiled surface and, with lightly oiled hands, knead the dough for 3 minutes until soft and elastic. You may need to add a little more oil if the dough starts to stick to the surface or your hands. Transfer to a lightly oiled bowl and cover with a clean, damp kitchen towel. Let rise in a warm place for 40 minutes, until nearly doubled in size.

2. Preheat the oven to 425°F.

3. Combine the hazelnuts and sesame seeds in a small bowl and set aside 1 tbsp.

4. On a lightly floured surface, roll the dough out into a 12 x 16-inch/30 x 40cm rectangle, so that the longest side is toward you, parallel to the work surface. Using a spatula, spread the dough with Nutella, leaving a ¾-inch/2cm border on the top edge. Sprinkle the orange zest evenly over the Nutella, then scatter the sesame seed and hazelnut mix on top. With the longest side still toward you, roll the dough into a long log. Brush with the remaining 1 tbsp of oil, then sprinkle on the remaining 1 tbsp of sesame seed and hazelnut mix (press them into the dough gently, so they stick). Trim the ends and cut the roll into 10 segments, each 1¼ inches/3cm long, and transfer to a parchment-lined baking sheet, seam side down.

5. Bake for about 10 minutes, until golden brown. Dust with the confectioners' sugar and let cool slightly. Serve.

Mint and pistachio chocolate fridge cake

Serves twelve

3½ oz/100g mint-flavored dark chocolate, roughly chopped into 1¼-inch/3cm pieces

7 oz/200g dark chocolate (70% cacao), roughly chopped into 1¼-inch/3cm pieces

8½ tbsp/120g unsalted butter, cut into ¾-inch/2cm cubes

2 tbsp light corn syrup

salt

¾ cup/100g golden raisins, soaked in 2 tbsp of rum for 30 minutes

6 oz/170g graham crackers, roughly broken into ¾-inch/2cm pieces

¾ cup plus 1 tbsp/100g shelled pistachios, chopped

This is called a chocolate fridge cake but it should be seen as a bit of a larder cake as well, using what you have on hand—which is why this is a pantry recipe. All sorts of different-flavored chocolate (ginger chocolate, chile chocolate, and so forth), nuts, dried fruit, or alcohol can be used, instead of what's listed here, depending on what you have and what you like. The cake can be stored in the fridge, in a sealed container, for up to 1 week.

1. Line a 8 x 10-inch/18 x 28cm baking pan or glass baking dish with parchment paper and set aside.

2. Put both chocolates, the butter, corn syrup, and ⅛ tsp salt in a large heatproof bowl set over a saucepan of barely simmering water (taking care that the base of the bowl is not touching the water). Heat for 2–3 minutes, stirring often, until completely melted and combined.

3. Add the raisins and rum, the graham crackers, and three-quarters of the pistachios (try adding the larger bits here, reserving the more powdery bits to finish) to the chocolate. Using a spatula, combine everything until the graham crackers and nuts are completely coated in chocolate. Transfer to the prepared pan, smoothing the top with the spatula so that it's flat and even, then sprinkle the remaining pistachios on top. Set aside for 10 minutes to cool, then wrap tightly with plastic wrap. Refrigerate for 2–3 hours, until completely set.

4. Cut into 24 bars. If not serving straightaway, store them in an airtight container and serve fridge-cold.

Brunsli chocolate cookies

Anyone from Switzerland will tell you that these should only be made with cinnamon and cloves and only baked and eaten at Christmas. Having played around with the spice mix and baked and eaten them happily throughout the year, I would make the case for the rules for this chewy brownie-like (and gluten-free) cookie to be extended. Swiss-born Cornelia Staeubli, through whom nearly all decisions at Ottolenghi have to pass, would firmly disagree! It's true, though, that they're particularly at home when things are festive, so I've made them into stars to play the game.

Either way, these keep for 5 days in a sealed container. The dough can also be frozen (either when shaped into a ball or cut into cookie shapes) for up to 1 month. If you bake from frozen, just add another 1–2 minutes to the cooking time.

Makes eighteen cookies (if using a 2¾-inch/7cm cookie cutter)

2¾ cups/270g almond meal

1¼ cups/250g granulated sugar, plus 1 tbsp to sprinkle on top

¼ cup plus 1 tbsp/ 40g confectioners' sugar, sifted

½ cup/40g Dutch-processed cocoa powder, sifted

1 orange: finely zest to get 1 tsp

1½ tsp Chinese 5-spice powder

¼ tsp salt

2 large egg whites

1 tsp vanilla extract

1. Preheat the oven to 375°F.

2. Place the almond meal, granulated sugar, confectioners' sugar, cocoa powder, orange zest, 5-spice powder, and salt in the bowl of a standing mixer fitted with the dough hook. Mix on medium speed, until combined. With the mixer running, add the egg whites and vanilla and continue to mix for 1–2 minutes, until the dough comes together into a ball. Tip the dough out on a clean surface, shape into a flat disk about 1¼ inches/3cm thick, and wrap in plastic wrap. Place in the fridge for about 1 hour, to rest.

3. Cut out two pieces of parchment paper, each 16 inches/40cm square. Unwrap the dough from its plastic wrap, place in the middle of the two sheets of parchment paper, and roll out to form a circle about 9 inches/22cm wide and ½ inch/1½cm thick. Using a 2¾-inch/7cm star-shaped cookie cutter (or whichever cookie cutter you are using), cut out the stars and place on a parchment-lined baking sheet. Press together the scraps of dough and roll out again, cutting out more stars. Continue until all the dough has been used, then sprinkle the tops with the 1 tbsp of granulated sugar.

4. Bake for 12 minutes, until the bottoms are slightly crisp and the middles are soft and gooey. Remove from the oven and set aside to cool.

No-churn raspberry ice cream

This is the same recipe for ice cream used in the Knickerbocker Glory in my book SWEET. It's a great stand-alone recipe, so here it gets its own page.

Make this throughout the year—fresh raspberries are great when they're in season and there is a glut, but frozen also work really well. The liquid released by the frozen kind actually gives the puree a lovely, smooth consistency. Get ahead with making this; it needs to freeze for at least 12 hours and both the ice cream and puree can be kept for up to 1 month.

Serves six

5 cups/600g fresh raspberries (or frozen and defrosted)

2 tbsp confectioners' sugar

¾ cup plus 2 tbsp/ 200ml heavy cream

1 egg, plus 2 egg yolks

1 tsp lemon juice

¾ cup plus 2½ tbsp/ 180g granulated sugar

⅛ tsp salt

1. Place the raspberries in a food processor and blitz to form a puree. Pass them through a fine-mesh sieve set over a bowl, using a large spoon to scrape the puree through the sieve to remove the seeds. Do this in batches if you need to. Measure out 1 cup plus 2 tbsp/260g of the puree and set aside. Sift the confectioners' sugar into the remaining puree—about ½ cup/100g—and decant into a jug. Keep in the fridge until ready to serve.

2. Place the cream in the bowl of a stand mixer fitted with the whisk attachment. Whip on high

speed until soft peaks form, then scrape into a bowl. Keep in the fridge until ready to use.

3. Fill a medium saucepan that your stand mixer bowl fits snugly over with enough water so that it rises ¾ inch/2cm up the sides without touching the base of the bowl. Bring the water to a boil, then decrease to a low simmer.

4. In the meantime, whisk together the egg, yolks, lemon juice, granulated sugar, and salt in a second mixer bowl. Place the bowl over the simmering water and whisk the mixture continuously for about 5 minutes, until the granulated sugar has dissolved and the mixture is very warm. Transfer the bowl to the mixer, fit the mixer with the whisk attachment, and beat on medium-high speed, until the mixture is thick and cooled. It will thicken quite quickly but takes about 10 minutes or more to cool. Add the 1 cup plus 2 tbsp/260g of puree and whisk on a low speed until combined. Scrape down the sides of the bowl and continue to mix until combined. Remove the whipped cream from the fridge and fold through to incorporate. Scrape the mixture into a large freezer container, cover the top with plastic wrap, and freeze for at least 12 hours.

5. About 10 minutes before serving, remove the ice cream from the freezer (so that it is soft enough to scoop). Divide among bowls and serve at once, with a drizzle of the reserved sweetened raspberry juice spooned over each portion.

SIMPLE Meal Suggestions
from midweek to weekend suppers

The number of ways in which 140 recipes can be combined to make various meals is large. Here are just a few meal-planning ideas covering a range of occasions, from quick midweek to special event or weekend suppers. In some instances there are several ideas, depending on the season. Focusing on the food that's in season and available is the best place to start in terms of keeping things simple in the kitchen and eating well. If a menu is vegetarian or vegan it will have a (V) or (VG) icon alongside.

Midweek supper

Spring/Summer

Avocado and fava bean mash, page 106 (the mash keeps for 2 days in the fridge; keep the fava bean and green onion garnish separate until serving) + **Couscous, cherry tomato, and herb salad, page 158** (all the elements can be made 1 day in advance) + **Beefsteak tomato carpaccio with green onion and ginger salsa, page 29** (make 6 hours ahead and keep in the fridge) (VG)

Stuffed zucchini with pine nut salsa, page 60 (the filling can be made up to 1 day ahead so that the zucchini are then ready to be stuffed and grilled) + **Baked mint rice with pomegranate and olive salsa, page 171** (make the salsa in advance, if you like—it will be fine sitting for a few hours) (V)

Shrimp and corn fritters, page 263 (the mix can be made up 1 day in advance and kept in the fridge until ready to fry) + **Herby zucchini and peas with semolina porridge, page 63**

Seeded chicken schnitzel, page 235 (the seed mix will keep for up to 1 month) + **New potatoes with peas and cilantro, page 147** + **Cucumber and lamb's lettuce salad, page 38** (prep the cucumbers and make the dressing, but keep separate until ready to serve)

Autumn/Winter

Curried lentil, tomato, and coconut soup, page 52 (make up to 4 days ahead) + **Tofu and haricots verts with chraimeh sauce, page 104** (the sauce will keep for 1 week) (VG)

Pumpkin, saffron, and orange soup page 54 (make the soup in advance and batch-cook the pumpkin seeds) + **Pappardelle with rose harissa, black olives, and capers, page 188** (make the sauce 3 days in advance) (V)

Chile fish with tahini, page 250
(make ahead or batch-cook both the tomato and tahini sauces as they keep well in the fridge or freezer) + **Fried broccoli and kale with garlic, cumin, and lime, page 75** *(blanch the broccoli and kale ahead of time)*

Pork with ginger, green onion, and eggplant, page 231 *(get all your chopping done before you start and this will be on the table in less than 15 minutes)* + **Plain rice or noodles** + **Broccolini with soy sauce, garlic, and peanuts, page 76**

Weekend brunch for friends

Pea, za'atar, and feta fritters, page 20 *(the batter can be made a day in advance)* + **Beet, caraway, and goat cheese bread, page 16** *(this keeps for up to 1 week—just slice and toast on the day)* + **Avocado and cucumber salad, page 13** *(this is the salad served with scrambled harissa tofu)* (V)

Scrambled harissa tofu, page 13 *(batch-cook the harissa onions and keep in the fridge)* + **Harissa-baked potato skins and crispy lettuce salad, page 146** *(use up potato skins or save the cooked flesh of a baked potato to make mash)* + **Nutella, sesame, and hazelnut rolls, page 286**

Weekend lunch and supper for friends

Spring lamb and sides

Slow-cooked lamb shoulder with mint and cumin, page 215 *(get the lamb marinating overnight in the fridge)* + **Baked mint rice with pomegranate and olive salsa, page 171** *and/or* **New potatoes with peas and cilantro, page 147** + **Cucumber and lamb's lettuce salad, page 38** *(make the dressing and prep the cucumbers)* and/or **Avocado and fava bean mash, page 106** *(the mash keeps for 2 days in the fridge)* + **Tomatoes with sumac shallots and pine nuts, page 34** *(the elements can all be made in advance)*

Summer salmon supper

Bridget Jones's pan-fried salmon with pine nut salsa, page 246 + **Aromatic olive oil mash, page 130** *(potatoes can be prepped in advance)* + **No-churn raspberry ice cream, page 292** *(this keeps well in the freezer, so it can be made in advance)*

Spring roast chicken and sides

Spring roast chicken with preserved lemon, page 227 (*the chicken can be prepped ahead, ready to go into the oven*) **+ New potatoes with peas and cilantro, page 147** (*this can be made a few hours in advance*) **+ Chopped salad with tahini and za'atar, page 36**

Autumn roast chicken and sides

Arnold's roast chicken with caraway and cranberry stuffing, page 219 (*stuff the chicken ahead of time, so it is ready to go in the oven*) **+ Aromatic olive oil mash, page 130** (*potatoes can be prepped in advance*) **+ Roasted baby carrots with harissa and pomegranate, page 116** (*the carrots can be roasted a few hours before serving*) **+ Cavolo nero with chorizo and preserved lemon, page 85**

Festive supper

Chicken Marbella, page 229 (*the chicken can be marinating up to 2 days ahead, ready to go into the oven*) **+ Baked rice with confit tomatoes and garlic, page 174 + Carrot salad with yogurt and cinnamon, page 118** (*steam the carrots in advance and add the herbs and yogurt before serving*) **+ Brussels sprouts with browned butter and black garlic, page 113**

Family supper

Gnocchi alla Romana, page 198 (*make this up to the point when it goes into the oven*) **+ Ricotta and oregano meatballs, page 221** (*make these ahead, ready to be warmed through in the oven before serving*) **+ Cucumber and lamb's lettuce salad, page 38** (*the dressing can be made 2 days in advance and kept in the fridge*)

Asian fish

Whole roasted sea bass with soy sauce and ginger, page 260 (*the whole dish can be prepared a few hours ahead, ready to go into the oven*) **+ Broccolini with soy sauce, garlic, and peanuts, page 76** *and/or* **Quick okra with sweet-and-sour dressing, page 86 + Thai sticky rice with crispy ginger, chile, and peanuts, page 173**

Feasts

Feasts, for me, are where you do most of the cooking in advance and then have a great spread of food to which people can help themselves. The recipes I go to when making a feast are those whose quantities can be easily doubled or tripled (or more) as needed. They're dishes that are happy to sit around for a while and be eaten at room temperature, when everyone is ready. Exceptions to this—when something needs to come out of the oven at the last minute or where assembly should be last minute—are noted where relevant. I've erred on the side of really covering the table in food here, but don't feel you have to cook everything listed for it to be a feast.

Tapas feast

See image on page 126–127

Avocado and fava bean mash, page 106 (the mash keeps for 2 days in the fridge; keep the fava bean and green onion garnish separate until serving) + **Lima bean mash with muhammara, page 107** (both elements can be made in advance and assembled before serving) + **Rose harissa chickpeas with flaked cod, page 262** + **Squid and red bell pepper stew, page 259** (make this up to 2 days in advance and warm through before serving) + **Oven fries with oregano and feta, page 138** (the potatoes can be parboiled in advance) + **Lamb arayes with tahini and sumac, page 214** (make the filling up to 1 day in advance)

Middle Eastern feast

See image on page 210–211

Grilled lamb fillet with almonds and orange blossom, page 208 (all the elements can be prepared in advance and assembled before serving) + **Couscous, cherry tomato, and herb salad, page 158** (all the elements can be made 1 day in advance) + **Green onion and herb salad, page 47** (make the dressing the day before and prep the salad 6 hours in advance, up to the point of adding the herbs and salt) + **Roasted beets with yogurt and preserved lemon, page 125** + **Roasted whole cauliflower, page 94** with **Green tahini sauce, page 95** (the sauce keeps well in the fridge for up to 3 days) + **Roasted baby carrots with harissa and pomegranate, page 116** (bake the carrots 6 hours in advance and assemble just before serving) + **Chopped salad with tahini and za'atar, page 36**

Spring lamb feast

See image on page 44–45

Slow-cooked lamb shoulder with mint and cumin, page 215 (*get the lamb marinating overnight*) + **Baked mint rice with pomegranate and olive salsa, page 171** (*make the salsa in advance so that the rice is ready to put in the oven*) + **Roasted asparagus with almonds, capers, and dill, page 82** + **Tomatoes with sumac shallots and pine nuts, page 34** (*the elements can all be made in advance*) + **Tomato and cucumber raita, page 30** (*this will keep in the fridge for 2 days*) + **Zucchini, thyme, and walnut salad, page 31** (*make the garlic oil ahead and prep the zucchini up to 6 hours in advance, but wait to add the seasoning and lemon juice until ready to serve*).

Summer vegetarian feast

See image on page 152–53

Burrata with grilled grapes and basil, page 43 (*marinate the grapes for up to 1 day and grill just before serving*) + **Hot, charred cherry tomatoes with cold yogurt, page 70** (*the tomatoes need to be served hot, but can sit in the marinade for up to 1 day*) + **Stuffed zucchini with pine nut salsa, page 60** (*make the filling in advance, ready to stuff the zucchini before baking*) + **Gem lettuce with fridge-raid dressing, page 37** (*the dressing can be kept in the fridge for 3 days*) + **Butternut squash with corn salsa, feta, and pumpkin seeds, page 122** (*the elements can all be made 1 day in advance and then assembled*) (V)

Winter feast

See image on page 78–79

Arnold's roast chicken with caraway and cranberry stuffing, page 219 (*the chicken can be stuffed the day before and kept in the fridge*) + **Harissa and confit garlic roast potatoes, page 142** (*confit garlic can be made 2 days ahead and the potatoes can be parboiled 6 hours in advance*) + **Cavolo nero with chorizo and preserved lemon, page 85** + **Mushrooms and chestnuts with za'atar, page 112** (*these need to be served straight from the oven, but can be prepared up to the point of adding the salt and pepper and going in the oven*) + **Fried broccoli and kale with garlic, cumin, and lime, page 75** (*blanch the broccoli and kale in advance*) + **Carrot salad with yogurt and cinnamon, page 118** (*steam the carrots 6 hours in advance and let them come to room temperature before serving*)

"Ottolenghi" Ingredients

These are the 10 ingredients I'm urging you to seek out and stock up on. Even though I've called them "Ottolenghi" ingredients they're not "mine," of course; they've all been around a lot longer than me! They are, however, things I love to cook with, rely on a lot in the kitchen, and will keep championing until, I hope, they become a lot of people's everyday ingredients.

As with all ingredients, there's a huge range in the quality of each product. Price is a guide—you tend to get what you pay for—but, more than this, buying something from the country of origin will always give you the more authentic (which often just translates as tastier) version of the product. The sharpest barberries will always be those from Iranian grocers, for example; the tartest sumac—as with the most aromatic za'atar and the creamiest tahini—will always be from a Middle Eastern store.

This is not to say that shopping for everything in one big supermarket—and buying the house brand version of things—is in any way wrong. It is to say, though (particularly if you live in a city or do your grocery shopping online) that it's worth taking a ten-minute detour to seek out a specialty shop to find these things or place an order online. We sell them at all our Ottolenghi shops, as just one example, as well as through our Ottolenghi web store.

Either way, and whatever version of the product you get hold of, these ingredients are all little flavor bombs, enriching and making bold whatever they're added to. They all have a long shelf life, too, so don't worry—you won't need to add black garlic to every dish you make for weeks once the container is open.

That being said, there are so many ways each ingredient can be used that you shouldn't be short of ideas as to what to do with them. Here are just a few ideas, both general and, specific to the recipes in *Ottolenghi SIMPLE*.

Barberries have an acidic tang that sweeter currants don't, and they work well with all sorts of fritters, frittatas, omeletes, and rice-based salads. There are only two recipes in *Ottolenghi SIMPLE* that call for barberries—the Iranian herb fritters (page 22) and the tomato, orange, and barberry salsa, which goes with the trout (page 248)—but, still, I think they're really worth having in your cupboard. If you don't have them, just soak an equal quantity of currants in a little bit of lemon juice—about 2 tbsp of lemon juice for 3 tbsp of barberries—for a half hour. These can then be drained and substituted for barberries.

Black garlic has a wonderfully concentrated flavor. The cloves start off as regular white garlic cloves that are then treated over a long period and allowed to ferment. If white garlic can be harsh (and make your breath smell), then these black cloves are the very opposite: mellow, sweet, and umami-rich. I've used them in *Ottolenghi SIMPLE* to take the bitter edge off some Brussels sprouts (page 113) and add their mellowness to an already-comforting brown rice dish (page 168), but play around with adding them to other recipes. Try adding a thinly sliced clove or two to your pizza before it gets baked, for example, or stirring some into a risotto.

Ground cardamom can be hard to find in the United Kingdom. Therefore, most recipes in *Ottolenghi SIMPLE* start with whole cardamom pods and work from there (getting you to bash the pods open and gently crush the seeds inside). Ground cardamom is easily available in the United States, so you may use it instead. It brings an aromatic and distinctive sweetness to all sorts of desserts and savory dishes. It's there in the soba noodles in *Ottolenghi SIMPLE*, for example (page 181), and in the salsa to go with the pan-fried mackerel (page 244). As a guide, if a recipe talks of ½ tsp of cardamom seeds (which you'd then crush yourself), you should use ¼ tsp of ground cardamom. Flavor bombs are one thing, but you don't want them to actually explode in your mouth.

Pomegranate molasses is syrupy, sweet, and sharp. Adding a drizzle to all sorts of meat or vegetable dishes is a way of injecting this welcome sweet-sharp note into the dish. The molasses pairs incredibly well with ground lamb, as just one example. I always find myself adding a little bit to the mix when I'm making meatballs (page 204) or a lamb mix to be piled into pita bread sandwiches (page 214). Adding a drizzle to a marinade or the base of a slow-cooked stew is also a very good way to create a sweet and sticky coating for whatever's being cooked.

Preserved lemon offers a real pop of citrus flavor. I often just chop the skin of a preserved lemon and add it to a dish or dressing to add a citrus hit. In *Ottolenghi SIMPLE*, I've used the small soft-skinned preserved lemons, rather than the larger thick-skinned ones, whose flavor is much more pronounced. Preserved lemon is used throughout the recipes here to bring a bite of contrast to an otherwise refreshing iceberg lettuce salad (page 146) or a tomato and cucumber raita (page 30), for example. It works just as well when cutting through earthy beet dishes (page 125) or keeping things vibrant in an otherwise comforting dish of braised eggs (page 6).

Rose harissa is a heavily spiced North African chile paste. I absolutely love it and it's used throughout *Ottolenghi SIMPLE* in all sorts of dishes—to marinate beef sirloin, for example (page 224), to rub over baked potato skins before they get roasted (page 146), to elevate a simple pasta dish (page 188) or omelete with Manchego (page 7), or to make a batch of caramelized harissa onions to spoon alongside a tasty brunch (page 13). The difference between harissa and rose harissa is the addition of the rose petals in the latter; generally speaking, they bring a special sweetness to the paste and soften the kick of the chile. That being said, the range in kick between one harissa and the next, or one rose harissa and the next can be absolutely huge. Recipes in *Ottolenghi SIMPLE* have been tested with Belazu rose harissa, which I really like. If you're starting with something else, then you'll need to taste what you have and gauge how much to use. A lot of supermarket brands aren't that punchy so you'll need to use 50 percent more than the recipe says. Much of the harissa or rose harissa that you buy from a North African shop, on the other hand, will have a really spicy kick so you'll need to use 50 percent less than the recipe says. With heat, it's always going to be a matter of taste and tolerance, so have a play around to see what works for you.

Sumac is the deep red ground spice made from the dried and crushed berries of the sumac shrub. The flavor is astringent and citrusy, and the spice can be sprinkled over all sorts of dishes. Eggs are a classic pairing, but it works just as well with grilled meat, fish, and vegetables. It can either be sprinkled over a dish as it is or mixed with some oil as the base for a dressing or marinade. Sumac onions (page 34) were something of an obsession for me one summer, when I couldn't stop piling them on top of sweet tomatoes, and I also like to make a sumac yogurt sauce (page 217) to serve with lamb patties or spoon over roasted vegetables. Sumac tends to be seen as savory but it does work in sweet dishes too (page 272).

Tahini is little more than an oily paste made up of ground sesame seeds, but still, the quality varies hugely depending on where and how it's made. Having grown up on it, I'm predisposed toward the creamy Lebanese, Israeli, and Palestinian brands rather than the Greek and Cypriot ones, which I find to be a bit claggy (mudlike) and not as flavorsome. Being less claggy, they pour well, so are ready to go into all sorts of dressings and sauces. I love to drizzle tahini over so many things. A simple chopped salad (page 36), for example, or into a dressing made with honey, mirin, soy sauce, and other ingredients for a seaweed and sesame salad (page 183). It's also great on toast—as you'd spread peanut butter, topped with honey or date syrup—or just drizzled over vanilla ice cream. Tahini is in so many *Ottolenghi SIMPLE* recipes, enriching the topping for a lamb meatloaf (page 212), drizzled lightly over some poached fish (page 250), or made into a green sauce to be served alongside roasted veg (page 95).

Urfa chile flakes are the type of chile flakes I reach for most days, although I use various chiles in my cooking. They are all about flavor—smoky and almost chocolate-like—rather than heat, so you can really be liberal with what they're sprinkled over. Try adding the flakes to scrambled eggs, smashed avocado on toast, or a cheese sandwich. In *Ottolenghi SIMPLE* I've sprinkled them over roasted cherry tomatoes, for example, warm from the oven (page 70), as well as on top of a Puy lentil and eggplant stew (page 159).

Za'atar is the green powder made from dried and ground za'atar leaves, sesame seeds, sumac, and salt. There's a huge range in the quality of available brands but I only like to use those with just these four ingredients in them. The leaves have a distinctive, savory aroma and their flavor is complex. There's a connection to oregano and marjoram, but also to cumin, lemon, sage, and mint. A pinch sprinkled over meat, fish, or vegetables, or mixed with oil and drizzled over dishes, can absolutely transform them. See the chopped salad with tahini and za'atar, for example (page 36), or the roast mushrooms and chestnuts (page 112). Za'atar is also great sprinkled over all legume-based spreads. If you don't want to make the red pepper paste to go on top of the lima bean mash (page 107), for example, then just a sprinkle of za'atar also works.

A note on vegetarian, vegan, and gluten-free recipes

This book is all about recipes that fit with in the *Ottolenghi SIMPLE* structure without any compromise on freshness, bounty, and flavor. Any other "free-from" focus was not, this time, a priority. I was delighted, therefore, to see how many of the recipes were still vegetarian and vegan. You'll see that 100 percent of the soups; raw veg; grain, rice, and pulse dishes; and desserts, for example, are vegetarian, as are 80 to 90 percent of the brunch, cooked veg, and potato dishes. Half of the potato and grain, rice and pulse recipes, and raw veg dishes are vegan.

Index

303

Acknowledgments

It is my name that appears on the cover of this book but there are two very important people who, really, deserve similar credit. Their distinct fingerprints can be found on every single page.

Tara Wigley has worked on a number of my books, always bringing in an unparalleled, thoughtful contribution. With *Ottolenghi SIMPLE*, her latest "baby," it was Tara who suggested breaking down the recipes into different kinds of "simple." Her experience as a cook as well as a talented writer was instrumental in giving this book its particular shape and flavor.

Esme Howarth, whose official job description as a recipe tester doesn't do justice to her real input, was involved in assessing, almost clinically, every dish that made the final cut. Her ideas are dotted throughout the book in the shape of complete recipes, as well as the different accents and light touches that make a good thing the best of its kind.

Thanks to Claudine Boulstridge, who cooked every single dish here, fed it to her family, and fed us constructive criticism. Thank you also to Ixta Belfrage for many a clever suggestion.

I am happy and grateful for my long-term collaboration with Jonathan Lovekin, who photographed the recipes, and Caz Hildebrand, who designed the book. Thank you both! And thank you, Wei Tang, for the plates, the props, and the two silver ducks.

Particular thanks to Noam Bar—for knowing and telling it as it is—and to Cornelia Staeubli and Sami Tamimi.

I would also like to express my gratitude to a bunch of people, on both sides of the Atlantic, who were crucial enablers: Felicity Rubinstein, Kim Witherspoon, Lizzy Gray, Louise McKeever, Rebecca Smart, Jake Lingwood, Mark Hutchinson, Gemma Bell, Sarah Bennie, Diana Riley, Helen Everson, Aaron Wehner, Lorena Jones, and Sandi Mendelson.

Thank you also to Gitai Fisher, Sarah Joseph, Bob Granleese, Melissa Denes, Josh Williams, and Nichole Dean.

Lastly, I want to thank my family and extended family: Karl Allen, Max, and little Flynn; Michael and Ruth Ottolenghi; Tirza, Danny, Shira, Yoav, and Adam Florentin; and Pete and Greta Allen, Shachar Argov, Helen Goh, Garry Chang, Alex Meitlis, Ivo Bisignano, Lulu Banquete, Tamara Meitlis, Keren Margalit, Yoram Ever-Hadani, Itzik Lederfeind, Ilana Lederfeind, and Amos, Ariela, and David Oppenheim.

Yotam Ottolenghi

Tara would like to thank the following for helping her out with their advice, appetites and support: Vicki Howard, Cornelia Staeubli, Carenza Parker, Sala Fitt, Suzanna and Richard Roxburgh, Alison and Alec Chrystal, Sophie O'Leary, and Chris Wigley. Vicki, for her advice (with the words); Cornelia, for her advice (with the everything); Carenza, for her appetite (for the food and washing up!); Sala, for her appetite (for the wine); Suzanna, Richard, Alison, Alec, and Sophie, for their support (with the kids); and Chris for all of the above and so much more.

Tara Wigley

Esme would like to thank: her husband, Mark Howarth, for his constant support and eager taste buds. Her enormous 39-week-old bump that let her off without too much morning sickness, so she could continue cooking and tasting during the making of this book. Her parents, Waring and Alison Robinson, for feeding all creativity in her life—especially her mother for her rice and dal lunches and delicious slow-cooked stews. All the friends and yachties she has fed over the years who have given advice, encouragement, and provided the freshest of fish. Lastly, the amazing Ottolenghi family, who could not be more supportive.

Esme Howarth

Ten Speed Press and the Ten Speed Press colophon are registered trademarks of Penguin Random House LLC.

Originally published in the United States in hardcover by Ten Speed Press, an imprint of Random House, a division of Penguin Random House LLC and in slightly different form in Great Britain by Ebury Press, an imprint of Ebury Publishing, Penguin Random House Ltd., London, in 2018.

Design by Caz Hildebrand, Here Design

10 9 8 7 6

2019 Trade Paperback Box Edition